Interpersonal
Communication

Current Continental Research
is co-published by
The Center for Advanced Research
in Phenomenology
and
University Press of America, Inc.

CURRENT CONTINENTAL RESEARCH 002

Joseph J. Pilotta
editor

INTERPERSONAL COMMUNICATION

Essays in Phenomenology
and
Hermeneutics

1982

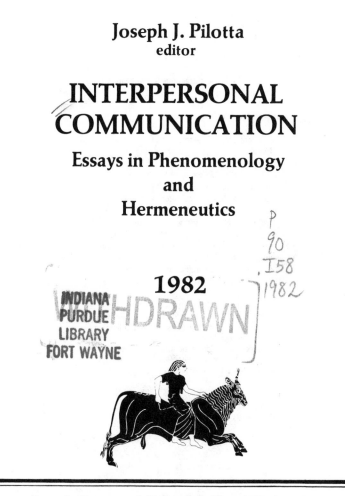

Center for Advanced Research in Phenomenology
& University Press of America, Washington, D.C.

Copyright © 1982 by
The Center for Advanced Research in Phenomenology, Inc.

University Press of America,® Inc.

4720 Boston Way
Lanham, MD 20706

3 Henrietta Street
London WC3E 8LU England

Printed in the United States of America

Library of Congress Cataloging in Publication Data
Main entry under title:

Interpersonal communication.

  (Current continental research ; 002)
  Includes eight papers presented at a
Symposium in Phenomenology and Hermeneutics
on May 17-18, 1978 sponsored by the Dept. of
Communication at Ohio University.
  Includes bibliographical references and
indexes.
  Contents: Hermeneutics and research in
interpersonal communication / Stanley Deetz —
Transcendental philosophy and human communi-
cation / Michael J. Hyde — Communicative
competence as a research criterion / Joseph J.
Pilotta — The dialogical region / Algis
Mickunas — [etc.]
  1. Communication—Philosophy—Congresses.
2. Interpersonal communication—Congresses.
3. Hermeneutics—Congresses. 4. Phenomenology—
Congresses. I. Pilotta, Joseph J.
II. Symposium in Phenomenology and
Hermeneutics (1978: Ohio State University)
III. Ohio State University. Dept. of
Communication. IV. Series.
P90.I58   001.51'01   82-40211
ISBN 0-8191-2475-3   AACR2
ISBN 0-8191-2476-1 (Pbk)

Preface

The Department of Communication at The Ohio State University sponsored a Symposium in Phenomenology and Hermeneutics on May 17-18, 1978. The purpose of this symposium was to introduce these approaches to the communication science field in the interest of developing qualitative orientations based on the logic of meaning. Within the course of the symposium, the themes emerged "what is interpersonal communication?; how can interpersonal communication be explicated through phenomenology and hermeneutics?; do other forms of communication presuppose interpersonal communication?"

These questions indicated a need to understand interpersonal communication, not only in a manner different than the traditional mechanical sender-receiver model, but as a quest to find a fundamental model for communication science. In order to address these questions and to provide a paradigm for interpersonal communication via phenomenology and hermeneutics, authors from The Ohio State Symposium have contributed to this collection. They are A. Lingis, S. Deetz, A. Mickunas, T. Seebohm, T. Widman, J. Pilotta, D. Ihde, and E. Behnke. In order to flesh out the interpersonal communication themes, D. Cegala, H. Silverman, and M. Hyde were asked as well to contribute to this project.

The social scientist and phenomenological philosopher, Alfred Schutz, has clarified the interpersonal theme which has served to organize this collection:

> The concrete researches of many sociologists and philosophers have aimed at certain forms of social intercourse which necessarily precede all communication. Wiese's "contact-situations," Scheler's perceptual theory of alter ego, to a certain extent Cooley's concept of the face-to-face relationship, Malinowski's interpretation of speech as originating within the situation determined by social interaction, Sartre's basic concept of "looking at the other and being looked at by the Other" (**le regard**), all these are just a few examples of the endeavor to investigate what might be called the "mutual tuning-in relationship" upon which all communication

is founded. It is precisely this mutual tuning-in relationship by which the "I" and the "Thou" are experienced by both participants as a "We" in vivid presence.[1]

The description by Schutz grounds the notion of communication as "mutuality." Mutuality is a relation which is not composed of two discrete ontological subjects, but is a "commonness." Phenomenologically, commonness emanates from the question of intersubjectivity or the experience of the other. The hermeneutical approach to commonness is secured through the medium of history consisting of a pre-given text in which humans find themselves. Hence, the structure of commonality or mutuality is fundamental to the interpersonal communication process. The communicative process is an orientation with the task of maintaining intersubjectivity.

The intersection of our actions in mutuality emerges from a background of a common life, constituting a common temporal field. We live in a temporal community in which the interpersonal present opens up toward a common past and future. A commonality constitutes itself when we bring forth something from our circumstances (horizons) in the present and open a common future and a common past. The object of communication may be theoretical, practical, or aesthetic, yet everything points to a "this-there" as an inescapable substrate of all communication. The "this-there" is an explicit understanding which is pre-given for such a distinction as "mine and yours" and allows the mutuality of both. Commonality is built up through the communalization of the immediately perceived. Commonality is actualized when the **same** aspect is "there" not only potentially but when we are motivated by the **same**. When our interests reply to the **same**, so that our orientations converge, then we can agree that we are dealing with the same (thing.) In this sense the world is **actually** common. In experience, one's own and the other's sensibilities pervade one another. Seeing, experiencing, and hearing are not contained in isolated subjects but I see and hear with the sensibilities of the other and the other with mine. The interpersonal world in the living present gains various sensibilities whereby each person can assume as well as change the sense. One looks from "there" and I look for "here" and the relationship institutes a mutual tuning-in where one and the other's sensibilities intersect.

Self and other experience are not disjunctive but accentuating moments of a total experience. The other points to me and I discover the other in myself. Therefore, the interpersonal communicative experience is a mutually changing acceptance

1. Alfred Schutz, "Making Music Together," COLLECTED PAPERS II, ed. Arvid Brodersen (Martinus Nijhoff: The Hague, 1964), p. 163.

and transmission. The essays in this collection unfold this interpersonal communication dynamic. Lingis gains access to the problem of commonness and Deetz reviews various approaches in the field of communication science. While many efforts at positivistic experimental research are limited, Cegala appropriates phenomenology as a supplement to this tradition. Moreover, the region of intersubjectivity as a common-life world is delineated by Silverman and is revealed as essentially a dialogical process by Mickunas. Seebohm explores the commonality of oral and written communication and their divergences. Widman picks up the hermeneutical theme to articulate the problem of history for the social sciences, based on the interpersonal model of H. G. Gadamer. The phenomenoloigcal and hermeneutical traditions are broached by both Hyde and Pilotta through a discussion of the transcendental region in communication. Technological mediation as a limitation of the interpersonal is discussed by Idhe, and Behnke develops a phenomenology of culture in which interpersonal paradigms are placed within an inter-cultural communication context.

Joseph J. Pilotta
Columbus, Ohio
March, 1982

Contents

Hermeneutics and Research in Interpersonal Communication

Stanley Deetz

The study of interpersonal interaction has been approached from many philosophical perspectives. Much of this research, however, has not explicitly discussed its own philosophical presuppositions. This lack of philosophical reflection has reduced much of the impact of interaction research. My interest is in establishing a foundation for research projects in interpersonal communication based in modern hermeneutics.[1] Included will be a discussion of some of the problems in recent interaction analyses and a consideration of the contribution hermeneutics might make to strengthen this work. This contribution will come through a reconsideration of basic concepts and through building a relation with the new types of research being conducted. While philosophical rigor is lost in doing applied studies, a careful grounding of these studies in sound philosophical frameworks is a key to their ultimate relevance and success.

As a communication researcher, I am committed to the thesis of complementariety.[2] Positivistic quantitative research is valuable when conducted with an awareness of its own limitations and with a respect for alternative forms of knowledge.

INTERPERSONAL COMMUNICATION: Essays in Phenomenology and Hermeneutics, ed., Joseph J. Pilotta, Copyright 1982, The Center for Advanced Research in Phenomenology, Inc. and co-published by arrangement with The University Press of America, Inc.

1. For a more detailed discussion of the theoretical and methodological issues involved see my "An Understanding of Science and a Hermeneutic Science of Understanding," JOURNAL OF COMMUNICATION, 23 (June 1973), 139-159; and, "Interpretive Research in Communication," JOURNAL OF COMMUNICATION INQUIRY, 3 (Summer 1977), 53-69.

2. See, Karl-Otto Apel, "The A Priori of Communication and the Foundation of the Humanities," MAN AND WORLD, 5 (1972), 3-37; and, Thomas Wilson, "Conceptions of Interaction and Form of Sociological Explanation," AMERICAN SOCIOLOGICAL REVIEW, 35 (1970), 697-709.

Phenomenological thought should add to the value of empirical research rather than replace it. Unfortunately the current popularity of phenomenological approaches has lead, at times, to a rejection of traditional quantitative research and a turn to overly romantic, subjective forms of phenomenology. We are, in a sense, caught between a rock and a soft place. The criticism directed here at traditional interpersonal communication' research is not intended to win converts, but to formulate a basis for additional research between the two extremes.

Interpersonal Communication Research

The study of interpersonal interaction is of considerable philosophical and social importance.[3] The interpersonal setting allows the most thorough mediation between the personal and the social. In the interpersonal dialogue the awareness of the reciprocity of collectivity and individuality is most clear. In the interpersonal context of the family, the child both becomes social and develops as an individual. All forms of social encounter, from reading to public speaking, follow after a person is a functioning interpersonal interactant. Reality construction, confirmation, and transformation principally take place in interpersonal interaction. In times of institutional breakdowns and legitimation crises, the interpersonal context becomes even more important.[4] In such times the social institutions are not fulfilling their meaning-validation function and interpersonal interaction is left to fill the gap. People talk to their friends about problems, parents educate their children, and one works for his/her boss rather than the company. The interpersonal encounter has a special residual capacity to support the individual and maintain identity and meaning.

Interpersonal communication involves the individual in the most thorough and integrated sense. The sheer physical presence of the interactant as well as her/his ability to object and amend make it difficult to define her/him in terms of institutional roles or generalized categories.[5] The physical traces of multi-dimensionality carried by the interactant reminds the other of the folly of uni-dimensional definitions and attributions of meaning.

3. Interpersonal communication and interpersonal interaction are used interchangeably here to suggest reciprocal, oral, face-to-face interaction.

4. Peter Berger, Brigette Berger, and Hansfried Kellner, THE HOMELESS MIND: Modernization and Consciousness (Random House, 1973).

5. Emmanuel Levinas, TOTALITY AND INFINITY, trans. Alphonso Lingis, (Pittsburgh: Duquesne University Press, 1969).

Interpersonal interaction also makes possible the use of all sense modalities. Within the interpersonal setting, it is difficult, if not impossible, to determine which modality is contributing which sense to the total message. Furthermore, such attempts would miss the point. The interpersonal message is precisely the synergy of all essential inputs. Analysis of interpersonal dialogue must recognize this synergy.

The special character and possibilities of the interpersonal setting are widely recognized. The interpersonal dialogue is often used as a metaphor for or a description of what interaction could be in its pure form. Nowhere is this clearer than in Gadamer's description of the genuine conversation.[6] The genuine conversation helps demonstrate what interpretive-understanding can be. The conversation, with its particular capacity for continuing **reply** epitomizes the dialectic revelation of truth. While Gadamer makes clear the particular advantages of a written text in interpretation, the special characteristics of interpersonal interaction are, to varying degrees, omitted or lost in other communication forms and settings. Understanding interpersonal interaction provides understanding of interpretation-understanding in all forms.

Unfortunately much of the work done concerning interpersonal interaction has missed this richness. In research interaction has been considered as a **dependent** variable in studies focusing on psycho-social independent variables. Much of the teaching about interpersonal interaction has developed out of humanistic psychology. Educational programs in interpersonal communication are highly subjective. Most center on an ego-centric philosophy concerned primarily with self-presentation.[7] Humanistic concepts, empathy training, and encounter groups are among the most visible parts of that tradition. Not only has the richness of interaction been missed, but the research itself has developed several problems.

First, most current research is conducted with inconsistent assumptions. While many of the concepts used in the research come out of a humanistic, processual tradition, many communication models and almost all the methodological guidelines have evolved out of a positivistic framework. Initially these positions may seem compatible. At some point, however, the

6. Hans-Georg Gadamer, TRUTH AND METHOD, ed. and trans. Garrett Barden and John Cumming (Seabury Press, 1975 [WAHRHEIT UND METHODE, 2 ed. (Tubingen: J.C.B. Mohr, 1965)]), pp. 325-341.

7. See the following discussions of dialogue: Richard Johannesen, "The Emerging Concept of Communication as Dialogue," QUARTERLY JOURNAL OF SPEECH, 57 (1971), 373-382; John Poulakos, "The Components of Dialogue," WESTERN SPEECH JOURNAL, 38 (1974), 199-212; and John Stewart, "Foundations of Dialogic Communication," QUARTERLY JOURNAL OF SPEECH, 64 (1978), 183-201.

researcher realizes that s/he is making assumptions about the nature of interaction which cannot be handled by the existing scientific concepts and methods. The inconsistency is clear in textbooks where the interaction process is described in one manner and supported by research findings based upon assumptions in direct opposition to those descriptions. Many researchers are aware of this problem, but it is not easily solved.[8] The methods and concepts are accepted, readily available, and give clear results; there are few available accepted methods which are consistent with the assumption that interaction is a processual phenomenon.

In addition, conceptual inconsistencies exist in the research. Communication researchers have borrowed concepts from a variety of disciplines. A borrowed concept carries its history—the theoretical assumptions, perspective, and system of distinctions out of which it is developed—implicitly into the research being conducted. The implicit character of this history allows for faulty juxtapositions of theoretical concepts. The borrowing of concepts must be accompanied by careful conceptual explication and active critical analysis. This has not been present in much of the research on interpersonal interaction. Often concepts developed from competing theoretical perspectives are used as primative terms, allowing both the researcher and the reader to combine conflicting technical and everyday meanings. The meaning of the research is consequently unclear and the research is almost impossible to productively criticize. Even when researchers are aware of the significance of their theoretical stances, when the research results are brought into the classroom and taught in a didactic fashion, the result is often more confusion. Students, who have not worked through the research step by step, have insufficient context from which to ascertain the significance of the research results.

Furthermore, little of the research has reached productive conclusions. Despite the many writings describing the importance of interpersonal communication, the social concern with interaction patterns and the laments over the decline of the family, neighborhood, and friendship, the research appears to have accomplished little regarding these concerns. The research reported is often interesting and relevant within its own world context; that is, to past research within a

---

8. Dennis Smith, "The Fallacy of the Communication Breakdown," QUARTERLY JOURNAL OF SPEECH, 56 (1970), 343-346; David Smith, "Communication Research and the Idea of Process," SPEECH MONOGRAPHS, 39 (1972), 1974-182; Daniel O'Keefe, "Logical Empiricism and the Study of Human Communication," SPEECH MONOGRAPHS, 42 (1975), 169-183; and Peter Monge, "The Systems Perspective as a Theoretical Basis for the Study of Human Communication," COMMUNICATION QUARTERLY, 25 (1977), 19-29.

particular paradigm within a particular research community.
The research is, however, narrow and serves more to show
the power of a research design or data reduction procedure
than to answer a significant question. The research appears
to generate numerous facts which have very meaning. The
results are fixed, replicable, and clear, but have little
appeal. Even applied research has tended to bring the lab
model into the life situation rather than adapting its methods
to that situation.

Despite important exceptions, much of the interaction research
today is abstracted from the life-world, inconsistant, and
without clear intent or purpose. In spite of the claims to
the contrary, the research is highly subjective. The concepts
and methods employed are largely determined by the researcher's training and preferences rather than by the nature
of the research problem. Little attempt is made to examine
the historical prejudices carried in these concepts and
methods. The "facts" created are largely artifactual--a quiet
reflection of the researcher and research tools. The "facts"
have little autonomy and capacity to interrogate human experience. Significantly, there is little reflexivity or social conceptual criticism.

The Conceptual Contribution to Hermeneutics

Hermeneutics is not the rabbit in the hat which is miracu-
lously going to appear to solve the problems discussed above
and to restore the study of interaction to its rightful place.
Hermeneutic thought does, however, have a role to play in
keeping open the possibilities fundamental to the interpersonal encounter and in establishing a basis for more productive research. Here I will briefly consider the most fundamental issues in current descriptions of interpersonal interaction, sketch a few guidelines for the development of hermeneutic methods for studying interpersonal interaction, and
discuss a few of the more positive directions of research in
interpersonal communication.

The assumed nature of intersubjectivity and human understanding are of great importance in the description of interaction. It is hard to imagine a careful study of interaction
which does not carry some theory of understanding or conception of how communication is possible. Yet there is little
evidence that most researchers have ever seriously considered
the question of how communication is possible.[9] Few

9. Lawrence Grossberg, "Intersubjectivity and the Conception of Communication," an unpublished paper presented at the annual meeting of the International
Communication Association, Acapulco, May, 1980.

definitions of communication have shown communication to be **possible** if the consequences of their basic assumptions about the nature of human consciousness are rigorously followed through. Theories of understanding have been proposed in communication literature.[10] But again there is little evidence that the research carried out ever takes into account the theory of understanding being assumed. Most researchers use "common sense" conceptions of intersubjectivity and the possibility of understanding. These positions contrast significantly with the careful hermeneutic position on these issues. Many of the problems with current research can be traced to an inadequate concept of intersubjectivity.[11] This reveals an inability to overcome dualism in both the research and in the descriptions of the interaction process.

Most communication researchers appear to work from one of two "common sense" positions on intersubjectivity. One position is best represented by the neo-positivists.[12] Essentially the problem of intersubjectivity is considered to be a problem of "other minds" and the possibility of understanding is generated out of the commonness of the empirical world and equivalence of the human sense equipment. Intersubjectivity is, in effect, reduced to objectivity. If people could learn to avoid prejudices, get rid of distortions, and see through to the **real** world, there would be little problem of understanding. The principle goal in studying communication would be to remove the prejudices which prohibit people from seeing the world as it is. With this position language is seen as the major prejudice. The popular general semantic phrases, "the word is not the thing," and "whatever you say the thing is, it isn't," best capture the sense of this position. Language is given a secondary status. It is a tool of thought--hopefully, a good, clean, careful tool. The scientist is presented as the model for all communicators. If people would all use operational definitons and be clearer and more precise, there would be fewer communication problems.

This position has paid off well for communication trainers. There are situations, in certain businesses, for example, in which communication interests are narrow and a strong desire to avoid possible misunderstandings is present. From a hermeneutic standpoint, this position is not wrong but derivative. It is dependent for its coherence upon more fundamental

10. David Berlo, THE PROCESS OF COMMUNICATION (Holt, Rinehart, and Winston, 1960), pp. 106-131.

11. Barry Brummett, "Some Implications of 'Process' or 'Intersubjectivity': Postmodern Rhetoric," PHILOSOPHY AND RHETORIC, 9 (1976), 21-51.

12. This position does not represent any particular philosophy, but represents an interpretation of philosophies presented in communication literature.

assumptions about the character of language, which it does not take into account. This derived view is based primarily on a philosophy of control.[13] The desire is for an administrative language which is given to a large number of people who reside in a world which is carefully controlled by those with the power of definition. While the definition is more often an unknown one, the shared common world is one defined by a set of political conditions which might not reflect the full potential of the society. If the goals of this position were reached (clear, precise communication), there might be fewer communication problems, but there would also be less to communicate about and we would only be expressing already shared meanings.

The other position on intersubjectivity assumed by people studying interpersonal interaction is based in modern humanistic psychology. This position is highly subjective. Each individual is assumed to have a private view of the world. Communication is a process of bridging the gap between these individual views. The basis for such a bridge rests in a collective unconsciousness, a mystic unity, or the human capacity to psychologically take roles. Since no two people have the same history, and consequently, no two people have learned to see the world in the same way, communication is inevitably incomplete. History is considered to be a form of personal background based upon psychological learning rather than as a cultural or social phenomenon. Language again plays a secondary role. Language is seen as abstract and only associated with experience through learning. Since each individual attaches words to somewhat different psychological experiences, understanding requires "getting behind" language. In an extreme form this position considers language to be an inadequate mode of expression. Language is social, thus is thought to distort the richness of personal experience. At best communication is a poor substitute for directly living through another person's experience.

Both of these largely derivative views of the relations among people, experience, and language have major flaws. In conceptualizing intersubjectivity, most communication researchers have started with a reasonable, but inadequate assumption. They assume that research must start with an individual who has an experience of others and the world. The concern is with the connections which must be made between the individual's experience and the other's experience and between the individual's experience and the world. The individual is seen as autonomous and needing self-directed effort to overcome this autonomy. From a phenomenological standpoint the

13. Herbert Marcuse, ONE DIMENSIONAL MAN (Beacon Press, 1964).

experience (the connection) is taken as the starting point. The entire view of intersubjectivity and understanding then shifts.

This change of focus has great consequences for the way that communication is studied, our understanding of research already conducted, and the definitions of the purpose of research. Since many of the papers in this volume discuss these issues in more detail, I will only mention the most basic parts of alternative positions.[14]

As Husserl made clear, subjectivity is intersubjectivity. Experience is not something a person has or makes up on her/his own. The individual finds her/himself in a world which is in language and is already structured. The experience one "has" is already social. The objects the individual sees are already named and distinguished in a language system which s/he did not create. It is difficult to imagine a viewpoint from which an individual could determine what is uniquely hers/his and what is social. People stand compresent to experience--as their own, everyone's and no one's--as a unity. The individual does not intend or create a world but is open to it. Language is central to this opening of world to experience. Self, other, and world retain their own particular autonomy, but an autonomy only understood in the context of their unity. The nature of successful communication is an allowing of this unity to show experience rather than an attempt to overcome the distance through intentional control.

A change in the conception of understanding in regard to communication naturally follows.[15] Most researchers have assumed a representational view of understanding. The listener is assumed to have understood when s/he can recreate what the speaker meant. The desire to avoid misunderstanding is central in this view. Modern hermeneutics demonstrates the possibility of a more productive view. The interest here in interpersonal interaction is with the development and unfolding of meaning which is not yet available to either interactant, rather than in a comparison of the speaker's psychological intentions with those of the listener. The nature of dialogue is to open that which is out of reach and beyond comprehension. Clarity and accuracy in the interest of productive understanding differs greatly from pursuing the same

14. Algis Mickunas, "The Dialogical Region," in this volume.

15. Stanley Deetz, "Conceptualizing Human Understanding: Gadamer's Hermeneutics and American Communication Studies," COMMUNICATION QUARTERLY, 26 (1978), 12-23.

in order to avoid misunderstandings.

As is clear in a hermeneutic description of intersubjectivity and understanding, the problems in current communication research will not disappear with more technological advancement in research procedures and data reduction techniques. This research directed at hypothesis-testing needs to be complemented by a more basic search procedure. Hermeneutic principles have offered much in cultural studies and in art, music, and literary criticism. While there are several remaining problems, hermeneutic-based analyses have potential for generating insight into the interpersonal process. Allow me to briefly sketch the task.

One reason for describing interaction is to bring into the open meaning which was present in the interaction but was overlooked. This was also the fundamental intent of psychoanalysis. This meaning is, however, much richer than that associated with unconscious motives, personal histories, or author's intent. This meaning is the interconnected set of experiential possibilities gathered as the linguistic tradition is expressed. The goal of research is to trace these interconnections and explicate the implicative structure which both makes meaning what it is and demonstrates its social significance. Fulfilling this task requires rigorous analysis.

The methodological intent of this analysis must be carefully understood. The mystical sound of some hermeneutic writings may invite passivity in potential researchers. In a weakened humanistic understanding, hermeneutics becomes a stance without a method, in which the researcher "waits for the world to speak." In some naturalistic circles, the image of the hermeneutic researcher is that of an intrigued child rather than a sage who has overcome the formulas of youth. Openness needs to be properly understood in hermeneutic research. Care and preparation are necessary. Productive research is more likely to come from those who incorporate current research tools yet go beyond them than from those who are untouched by traditional concepts and methods. Such research can only happen with an articulation of appropriate conceptual and methodological guidelines. Only the most basic principles have been developed in a form useful to analyzing everyday interaction.[16]

16. Joseph Kockelmans, "Toward an Interpretative or Hermeneutic Social Science," NEW SCHOOL GRADUATE FACULTY PHILOSOPHY JOURNAL, 5 (1975), 73-96.

Recent Interpersonal Communication Research

Several theoretical perspectives have been developed during the last ten years which promise to overcome the conceptual and methodological problems which have plagued traditional interpersonal interaction research. These positions both have more potential and are more likely to gain from the developments in hermeneutics. Three of these positions warrant some discussion here. They are conversational analysis, cognitive structure analysis, and interactional process analysis. I will briefly describe each position and discuss the contribution hermeneutics can make to it.

The most diverse group of new work falls in what I have called conversational analysis. This work can also be described as "rule analysis" since the work is tied together as much by what it is looking **for** as what it is looking **at**. The major theoretical issues and findings of this work are summed up in a recent book by Shimanoff.[17] As is clear from her work, most of the researchers have treated conversation rules as normative principles which explain action rather than following the conception of rules in linguistics. Rules, in this sense, are either formal statements of typified social action as in "turn-taking" or socially preferred action such as the use of forms of address. Rules, thus, describe surface feature regularity by appeals to conventional social processes rather than to law-like necessity or sign systems. This line of research attempts to avoid speaker meaning yet documents the need to consider extra-textual taken-for-granted knowledge and interlocutor interpretation. The normative conception of rules is actually not basic enough to describe the fundamental nature of interaction. At a minimum rules need to be conceptualized as interpretive rather than normative, that is, connected to the intelligibility of expression rather than its propriety. Rules, then, would specify the internal sense of a text rather than the conditions influencing its produced form.

Much of the difficulty stems from an inadequate concept of text and the treatment of the surface features of transcribed discourse as data. The recent discussions of textuality in hermeneutics could help greatly.[18] What is the text of interpersonal interaction? Interpersonal interaction has an oral

17. Susan Shimanoff, COMMUNICATION RULES: Theory and Research (Sage Publishing Company, 1980).

18. Richard Palmer, "What Are We Doing When We Interpret a Text?" EROS: A Journal of Philosophy and the Literary Arts, in press; and Samuel Ijsseling, "Hermeneutics and Textuality: Questions Concerning Phenomenology," RESEARCH IN PHENOMENOLOGY, 9 (1979).

rather than written "text." Several hermeneutic discussions have demonstrated essential differences between oral and written texts.[19] In analyzing oral discourse, there is no artifact to return to. This problem is aggravated further by the multiple authorship of the interaction and the lack of specific setting cues. These problems are not solved by modern technology. A videotape stands as a report of an interaction, not as the interaction itself. Even if the taping does not change what the interactants do, the tape replay of the interaction has a different character than the interaction itself. Interaction is private, fluid, and characterized by its association with the actor as well as by its forgetfulness. The tape replay is public, distant, and permanent. A good written description might be better at describing the interaction than the videotape. The experience of analyzing a videotape is more akin to film criticism than analyzing interaction. Yet the videotape is quite unlike the film. The film, like other artistic and literary forms, has a public intent. It is regarded as an attempt at importance. The displayed images are selected for a public. An interaction being taped is characterized by its commonness and its ordinary nature: it is for itself rather than for making **comment** on the ordinary. The videotape captures an uncertain, passing moment which, once removed, is difficult to contextualize either in the life of individuals or in the cultural matrix.

A recent interpersonal communication theorist has broken part of the difficulty. Hawes attempted to follow Heidegger in considering talk ontologically.[20] In his conversation analysis he examined how talk constitutes reality and a context for itself. His work is one example of how a particular line of work can be influenced by hermeneutics. While he might be somewhat overly zealous in describing originary qualities to everyday talk (a point neither defensible by reference to Heidegger or observation), the potential for contribution is clear.

A second, more unified, line of interaction research has developed from George Kelly's personal construct theory. Labeled as constructivist or cognitive developmental, the work discusses the structure and content of cognitive systems. Research has considered a large number of topics relevant to social interaction including social perspective-taking (role-

19. Paul Ricoeur, INTERPRETATION THEORY: Discourse and the Surplus of Meaning (Fort Worth, Texas: Texas Christian University Press, 1976); Ricoeur, "The Model of the Text: Meaningful Action Considered as a Text," SOCIAL RESEARCH, 38 (1971), 529-562; and Seebohm in this volume.

20. Leonard Hawes, "Toward a Hermeneutic Phenomenology of Communication," COMMUNICATION QUARTERLY, 25 (1977), 30-41.

taking), message adaptation, and relational development.[21]
Delia in particular has demonstrated considerable awareness
of the social and philosophical context for his work. There
is little doubt that this line of research will continue to have
considerable influence. The cognitive orientation, however,
has made better explanations of individual choices in interaction than of interaction characteristics themselves. If interpretation was understood hermeneutically (as the basic lin-
guisiticality of all experience) rather than psychologically
(as thought by virtue of cognitive categories), much of the
same analysis could be used but more easily expanded to
look at aspects of interaction. Cognitive structure is "read"
textually rather than mentally. The newest cognitive theories,
e.g., Streufert and associates, place much more emphasis
on interactive complexity considering complexity external to
the person's cognitive system.[22] The need for phenomenological concepts and data are clear in this move. Bannister and
others have shown the compatability of phenomenology with
traditional cognitive analysis. The connection waits to be
carefully worked out.

A third new approach is interactional process analysis. This
work, following Ruesch, Bateson, Watzlawick, and others,
emphasizes the systemic nature of human interaction.[23]
The systems analogue allows the most complete non-linear
analysis of interaction patterns available today. Much of
the research carried out from this perspective, however,
attempts to specify observational qualities of different relational patterns and relate them to external variables rather
than carry through the systems model. This is both less
useful and weaker theoretically. The development of hermeneutic
analytic procedures would aid in allowing the systems conception to be maintained while engaging in systematic study.

One of the most difficult features of the interactional process
is the multiple levels of meaning simultaneously present. The
multiple levels of meaning which have defied description by
traditional research ought to be a problem for hermeneutics

21. Jesse Delia, "Constructivism and the Study of Human Communication,"
QUARTERLY JOURNAL OF SPEECH, 63 (1977), 68–83; and Steven Duck, PERSONAL
RELATIONS AND PERSONAL CONSTRUCTS (Wiley, 1973).

22. Siegfried Streufert and Susan Streufert, BEHAVIOR IN THE COMPLEX
ENVIRONMENT (John Wiley, 1978).

23. Jurgen Ruesch and Gregory Bateson, COMMUNICATION: The Social Matrix
of Psychiatry (W.W. Norton and Company, 1951); Gregory Bateson, STEPS TO AN
ECOLOGY OF MIND (New York: Ballantine Books, 1972); and Paul Watzlawick,
Janet Beavin, and Don Jackson, PRAGMATICS OF HUMAN COMMUNICATION (New York:
W.W. Norton and Company, 1967).

par excellence. Unfortunately traditional hermeneutics has been content centered also. Hermeneutics has an unclear application to other dimensions of meaning in the interpersonal situation. Gadamer's discussion of the genuine conversation focused on **what** the conversation was about. All interpersonal interactions have meaning dimensions beyond content and many have a heavy emphasis on relational concerns. The content-relationship message distinction, made clear by Bateson and others, has become very important in the study of interaction. The process of exploring relational forms differs greatly from looking for symbolism or implicit meanings. Philosophical analyses formulating the ideal speech situation and concentrating on the nature of true dialogue have described the interactants as interchangeable, with equality between interactants the dominant relational form. In most human interactions, however, the people involved have essentially different rights and obligations. Even when they are equal, each person may play different roles. The relationship is not reducible to mere power and control, and it is an intrinsic part of the experience of interacting with another.

Recent interpersonal communication studies have expanded upon the concept of differing dimensions of meaning. The text is composed of several codes. At least four simultaneous meaning dimensions may be identified:

> (1) Content Dimension—What the interaction is about.
>
> (2) Perspectival Dimension—Placing the content in a particular word field, thus extending its linguistic possibilities and experiential character.
>
> (3) Relational Dimension—Defining the relative rights and obligations of the interactants.
>
> (4) Affective Dimension—Structuring the mood or orientation to the entire message structure.

In analysis, all four dimensions seem necessary to describe the interaction as it unfolds. One wonders in looking at each of these message structures whether an individual hermeneutic is needed for each dimension.

There are, of course, many other approaches to interaction research and several hybrids of those presented here. Of these the most significant for communication study has been developed by Pearce.[24] His position has an extremely carefully developed philosophical and empirical base. Discussion

24. W. Barnett Pearce and Verson Cronen, COMMUNICATION, ACTION, AND MEANING: THE CREATION OF SOCIAL REALITIES (Praeger, 1980).

of the relation of hermeneutics to it is beyond the scope of this paper.

Summary

Interpersonal interaction is highly important in today's society and is in much need of study. Much of the current research is based upon outdated conceptualizations of communication. Many of the research findings have been largely irrelevant. Careful philosophical analysis can help both to expose and resolve part of these difficulties. Hermeneutics offers alternative conceptions of intersubjectivity and human understanding thus changing the most basic description of the communication process. These concepts, plus methodological guidelines and interpretive research procedures, provide a positive groundwork for new research in interpersonal communication. Hermeneutic descriptions of "texts" and "interpretation" can potentially contribute to further development of the most recent approaches to communication study.

Transcendental Philosophy and Human Communication

Michael J. Hyde

In his recent book, **Radical Reflection and the Origin of the Human Sciences,** Calvin Schrag explores what he terms "the evident crisis in the current sciences of man." According to Schrag, "The human sciences comprise a tottering Tower of Babel in which each speaks with its own tongue, producing a virtual breakdown of communication not only among the several human sciences themselves but also within the republic of human knowledge more generally. Their accelerated development within recent years has produced such a proliferation of portraits and models of man that the common center from which they allegedly proceed is no longer recognizable."[1] Schrag identified this "common center" or "origin" of the human sciences with "the originary world of pure experience," "the precategorical domain of knowledge and human interests" wherein people first come to understand, interpret, and give meaning to the world, and which provides the "source of all constructionist designs, methodological and metaphysical."[2] As the human sciences have allowed "the question of utility and technique" to congeal "into a dogmatic assertion of epistemological first principles," the question of this "source" has become occluded by "the primacy of methodology"; hence, the crisis.

To remedy this crisis, Schrag argues, requires a returning to the source from which arises the intended phenomena of the human sciences. The source, and not the methodological

INTERPERSONAL COMMUNICATION: Essays in Phenomenology and Hermeneutics, ed., Joseph J. Pilotta, Copyright 1982, The Center for Advanced Research in Phenomenology, Inc. and co-published by arrangement with The University Press of America, Inc.

1. Calvin O. Schrag, RADICAL REFLECTION AND THE ORIGIN OF THE HUMAN SCIENCES (Purdue Univ. Press, 1980), p. ix.

2. Ibid., p. 102.

procedures of a particular scientific perspective or philosophy, must be acknowledged as that which informs both the phenomena and the construction of methodologies used to investigate the phenomena; for is not any methodology employed by the human sciences but a sophisticated interpretive scheme for analyzing that which is itself a process of interpretation, i.e., the world of everyday human affairs? Answering this question in the affirmative, Schrag formulates a "demand for reflexivity" as a corrective against the primacy of methodology. That is, methodological procedures, given their interpretive nature, must be instructed by that which they are and by that which they investigate--the process of interpretive understanding and meaning-formation which organizes the originary world of pure experience into the phenomena of human existence. Schrag notes:

> As such, reflexivity neither invalidates methodology nor does it legislate a nomethetic methodological rule for all the human sciences. It allows for a plurality of methodologies. There are many ways of seeing the world, and there are many ways of doing science and philosophy. What is required is that the methodological principles that inform the doing of science and philosophy not sever the phenomena from the method. . . . The ongoing self-interpretation within human motivation, thought, and action should solicit the method; the method should not prejudice the phenomena. If the origins are not to be occluded, the phenomena should be permitted to speak for themselves and thus guide the construction of methodological theory and procedure. The consequences of this rejection of the primacy of methodology is that methodology is no longer the absolute presupposition of inquiry but is itself a part of the "experimental" furniture.[3]

That Schrag's observations are significant for the field of communication is suggested by B. Aubrey Fisher. According to Fisher, communication scholars within the United States "have placed too much emphasis" on questions concerning the primacy of methodological procedures for investigating human communication phenomena. "The result," argues Fisher, "has been a continual internal squabbling over whose approach to the study of communication is better, which techniques are more 'scientific,' which 'theory' is better--in short, quibbling and nit-picking with no results other than shortened tempers."[4] As Fisher states it, "Such arguments from synonymy are inexcusable and represent intellectual bigotry at its worst."[5]

3. Ibid., p. 102-03.

4. B. Aubrey Fisher, PERSPECTIVES ON HUMAN COMMUNICATION (New York: Macmillan, 1978), pp. v-vi.

5. Ibid., p. 323.

Cognizant of this developing state of affairs within the field of communication, various communication scholars have sought remedial directives emerging from continental philosophy. Here, particularly in the works of Martin Heidegger, Hans-Georg Gadamer, Paul Ricoeur, Jürgen Habermas, Karl-Otto Apel, and Jacques Lacan, are contained philosophies of communication that posit ways for "returning" to the "source" or "transcendental ground" of human communication.[6] Although important differences exist between these philosophers concerning how this transcendental ground should be grasped for the purposes of communication research, all of these scholars have acknowledged what Heidegger, in his **Being and Time**, argued to be the transcendental ground of human communication: namely, the **a priori** conditions of interpretive understanding from which arises the experiential form of meaning and from which people come to know the world in and through their intrapersonal and interpersonal communicative experiences.

While communication scholars in the United States have offered various discussions of how the philosophies of communication contributed by Heidegger and his contemporaries can help transcend the methodological difficulties confronting the field today,[7] none have set forth a specific examination of the transcendental argument underlying each of these philosophies. The role of the transcendental in human communication must be realized if the efforts of communication researchers echoing its directives are to be fully appreciated and not falsely condemned by those who naively believe that only scientific results will show researchers "the way to the promised land."[8] Hence, the purpose of this essay is to clarify the role of the transcendental in human communication, especially as this role is described by Heidegger. Since the process of human communication is one wherein people engage in an

6. See, for example, Martin Heidegger, BEING AND TIME, tr. John Macquarrie and Edward Robinson (Harper & Row, 1962); Hans-Georg Gadamer, TRUTH AND METHOD, ed. Garret Barden and John Cumming (Seabury, 1975); Paul Ricoeur, THE CONFLICT OF INTERPRETATIONS, Essays in Hermeneutics, ed. Don Idhe: Northwestern Univ. Press, 1974); Jürgen Habermas, KNOWLEDGE AND HUMAN IN-TERESTS, tr. Jeremy J. Shapiro (Boston: Beacon, 1972); Karl-Otto Apel, TOWARDS A TRANSFORMATION OF PHILOSOPHY, tr. Glyn Adey and David Frisby (Routledge and Kegan Paul, 1980); and Jacques Lacan, ECRITS, A SELECTION, tr. Alan Sheridan (W.W. Norton, 1977).

7. Leonard C. Hawes, "Toward a Hermeneutic Phenomenology of Communication," COMMUNICATION QUARTERLY, 25, No. 3 (1977), 30-41; Stanley Deetz, "Conceptualizing Human Understanding: Gadamer's Hermeneutics and American Communication Studies," COMMUNICATION QUARTERLY, 26, No. 2 (1978), 12-23; the JOURNAL OF THE AMERICAN FORENSIC ASSOCIATION, 16, No. 2 (1979). Also see my "Jacques Lacan's Psychoanalytic Theory of Speech and Language," QUARTERLY JOURNAL OF SPEECH 66 (1980), 96-108.

8. Gerald R. Miller and Charles R. Berger, "On Keeping the Faith in Matters Scientific," WESTERN JOURNAL OF SPEECH COMMUNICATION 42 (1978), 44-57.

understanding of their world so as to interpret this understanding in a meaningful way, and since human communication
phenomena show themselves in and through this process of
"understanding-interpretation-meaning," an exploration of
Heidegger's transcendental argument can provide a way for
communication researchers to meet the "demand for reflexivity"
necessary for a "radical" grounding of communication theory.

To orient the reader in understanding Heidegger's transcendental argument, section one of this paper offers a clarification of the concept "transcendental." This clarification is
achieved by tracing a line of philosophical thought emerging
with Kant and evolving through Hegel, Kierkegaard, and
Husserl. Elucidated in the writings of these four philosophers
is a conception of transcendental that is fundamental to
Heidegger's understanding of its scope and function. Section
two provides an investigation of how the concept of transcendental is formulated by Heidegger. Finally, in section three,
implications of the present study for human communication
research are discussed.

What is Meant by the Concept "Transcendental"?

Kant's use of the term transcendental arose in his struggle
to explore the limits of reason and to show how metaphysics
as a science is possible. Kant argued that when metaphysics
is shown to be a science, the limits of reason must lie within
the "fruitful bathos" of actual experience; that is, the limits
must be of a transcendental nature. As Kant explained it,
the word transcendental signifies something that precedes
existence, an **a priori** condition which makes knowledge of
experience itself possible. When "conceptions overstep experience, their employment is termed 'transcendent,' which must
be distinguished from the immanent use, that is, use restricted
to experience."[9] For Kant, the origin of the transcendental
is the innate principles of thought that he labeled the "transcendental system." The transcendental system is, simply stated,
the **a priori** principles of thought which do not derive their
laws (**a priori**) from, but prescribe them to, nature.[10]
According to Kant, this transcendental system constitutes a
universal of nature and thus makes universal judgments possible (e.g., that 'A straight line is the shortest distance
between two points').[11] Being a universal, the transcendental system cannot be known as an "in-itself." Its different

---

9. Immanuel Kant, PROLEGOMENA TO ANY FUTURE METAPHYSICS, ed. L.W. Beck
(Bobbs-Merrill, 1950), note 2, pp. 122-123.

10. Ibid., pp. 30-31.

11. Ibid., p. 49.

principles can be represented only through logical proofs confirming their existence. Kant attempted these proofs through his "Transcendental Deduction."[12] For Kant, then, the limits of reason are: (1) the transcendental system which organizes all conscious activity of empirical experience into a "unity of self-consciousness," and (2) experience itself. When reason transcends these limits in its quest for absolute knowledge (e.g., a knowledge of God), reason according to Kant, becomes illusionary.

Kant's transcendental philosophy is recognized as an "ancestor" to Hegel's doctrine of Spirit in that both agreed that the "'self,' to which all thinking acts are referred, has no content whatever beyond the unifying, categorizing functions present in all thinking."[13] But Hegel took exception to Kant's argument concerning the limits of reason. This exception is dramatized in Hegel's development of his dialectical "system." Hegel advanced his system as a method for illustrating how a human being (as "finite consciousness") comes to know his/her "Thinking in its truth." For Hegel, the epistemological "goal to be reached is the mind's insight into what knowing is."[14] By acquiring such insight, Hegel believed (contra Kant) that God, as the Absolute Spirit (or Absolute Reason), could be grasped as a wholeness through a dialectical progression of thought. Hegel's statement that "truth is the whole" epitomized this belief. Thus, Hegel contended that what Kant described as "transcendence" is itself a part of the transcendental realm of human experience: the Absolute spirit (the "Universal in action") can be known by a finite being.

Kierkegaard's concern for understanding the limits and function of human reason—especially as they instruct humans about their "ethical" relationship to God—places him in the company of Kant and Hegel. Unlike his predecessors, however, Kierkegaard did not offer an explanation about the mind's transcendental constitution; rather, he concerned himself with elucidating the human "existential situation" wherein all reason arises when one reflects "existentially on the structure of existence in his own existence."[15] According to Kierkegaard, the fact that humans must "always reason from existence" defines all of life's situations as existential; one's life

12. Immanuel Kant, CRITIQUE OF PURE REASON, tr. F. Max Muller (MacMillan, 1966), pp. 69ff.

13. J.N. Findlay, HEGEL: A Re-examination (Humanities Press, 1970), p. 49.

14. G.W.F. Hegel, THE PHENOMENOLOGY OF MIND, tr. J.B. Baillie (Harper & Row, 1967), p. 90.

15. Sören Kierkegaard, CONCLUDING UNSCIENTIFIC POSTSCRIPT, tr. David F. Swenson and Walter Lowrie (Princeton University Press, 1971), p. 78.

situations taken as a whole are his/her existential situation. For Kierkegaard, this existential situation is not something that one must demonstrate to be--it is the transcendental ground, the **a priori** condition, from which people must reason out the "truth" of their world-view in "subjective" moments of enlightenment.[16] Kierkegaard summarized his argument as follows: "Thus I always reason from existence, not toward existence, whether I move in the sphere of palpable sensible fact or in the realm of thought. I do not for example prove that a stone exists, but that some existing thing is a stone. The procedure in a court of justice does not prove that a criminal exists, but that the accused, whose existence is given, is a criminal. Whether we call existence an accessorium or the eternal prius, it is never subject to demonstration."[17] Here Kierkegaard sides, in part, with Kant's philosophy; for Kierkegaard believed, like Kant and unlike Hegel, that reason always is limited by existence; to exist is to be separated always from "the knowledge of the eternal truth." Transcendence, or what Kierkegaard called the "leap of faith," is what moves finite reason toward the infinite (God). Consequently, Hegel's systematic development of reason becoming one with God struck Kierkegaard as utterly absurd. God's transcendence can never be equated with the transcendental nature of human existence. To make such a claim, argued Kierkegaard, is to forget "what it means to exist."[18]

Kierkegaard's writings produced the rise of modern **existentialism**. Husserl's critique of this doctrine as pure "irrationalism," along with his critique of nineteenth century positivism, resulted in a redefining of the transcendental ground of human experience. Husserl's conception of this transcendental ground takes form in his philosophy--**phenomenology**. For Husserl, phenomenology denoted both an "attitude of mind" and a corresponding "method" of philosophical investigation that substantiates such an attitude.[19] Simply stated, this attitude of mind maintains that "intentionality" (i.e., the movement of consciousness towards the objects of experience) is the **a priori** condition for all human experience; intentionality is the "invariant feature" of the experiential world. Husserl argued that only through an investigation of the workings of consciousness could philosophy become a "rigorous science." From this argument Husserl concluded that

16. See Kierkegaard, pp. 169ff.

17. Sören Kierkegaard, PHILOSOPHICAL FRAGMENTS OR A FRAGMENT OF PHILOSOPHY, tr. David F. Swenson (Princeton University Press, 1952), pp. 31-32.

18. Kierkegaard, CONCLUDING UNSCIENTIFIC POSTSCRIPT, p. 184.

19. Edmund Husserl, THE IDEA OF PHENOMENOLOGY, tr. William P. Alston (Martinus Nijhoff, 1973), pp. 18-19.

"the evidence of world-experience would . . . need to be criticized with regard to its validity and range, before it could be used for the purposes of a radical grounding of science, and that therefore we . . . must not take that evidence to be, without question, immediately apodictic. . . . The being of the world, by reason of the evidence of natural experience, must no longer be for us an obvious matter of fact; it too must be for us . . . only an acceptance-phenomenon" contingent on the workings of consciousness.[20]

To accomplish the requirements of this attitude of mind wherein he could establish what he called the "transcendental purity" of the thinking ego, Husserl prescribed a method for investigating the workings of consciousness. This phenomenological method was inspired by Descartes' philosophy of radical doubt in that Husserl, like Descartes, turned to the **Cogito** as the starting point of his investigations. But whereas Descartes was content to admit that the "I think" was the transcendental foundation of experience, Husserl was not. For Husserl, Descartes did not carry his transcendental deduction of the world far enough: Descartes failed to include in his equation of the **Cogito** the **reflexive** consciousness that would have enabled him to investigate the function and supposed certitude of the "I think." According to Husserl, the **Cogito** of Descartes must itself be reduced if the conscious workings of the "I think" are to show themselves. This further reduction, which Husserl called the "epoché," was for him the proper way to look at consciousness itself. The epoché places the thinker in a position to think about consciousness as it actually is occurring. As Husserl stated it, through the epoché,

> I reduce my natural human Ego and my psychic life--the realm of my **psychological self-experience**--to my transcendental-phenomenological Ego, the realm of **transcendental-phenomenological self-experience**. The Objective world, the world that exists for me, that always has and always will exist for me, the only world that ever can exist for me--this world, with all its Objects, . . . derives its whole sense and its existential status, which it has for me, from me myself, from me as the transcendental Ego. . . .[21]

Husserl claimed that the transcendental ego "is not a piece of the world"; rather, it is what makes a knowledge of the world possible. This conception of the transcendental ground of human experience suggested to many philosophers that Husserl was visualizing a "philosopher's god" whose certitude

20. Edmund Husserl, CARTESIAN MEDITATIONS: An Introduction to Phenomenology, tr. Dorian Cairns (Martinus Nijhoff, 1973), pp. 17-18.

21. Ibid., p. 26.

was doomed to a theological infinite regress.[22] Others, however, were more sympathetic to Husserl's task. As Natanson explained it, Husserl's search for and discovery of the transcendental ego enabled him to clarify what he considered to be the fundamental grounds of philosophical inquiry, to make explicit the requirements of philosophical method, and to illustrate the type of involvement needed by the thinker who desires to philosophize "about the everyday world in which he inhabits and whose demands embrace him."[23]

Husserl's phenomenology was transcendental in that it not only sought to uncover the a priori conditions of human experience but, in so doing, it also integrated its results and its method wherein its own methodology could be critiqued. Specifically, by arguing that consciousness is the invariant feature of all experience, and by constructing a method wherein the investigative tool became an analytically trained consciousness, Husserl elucidated that feature of experience that could be used to critique itself. This "self-referentiality" (or "reflexivity") of phenomenology enabled Husserl to make a transcendental claim for his philosophy that was beyond the scope of his predecessors' philosophies: phenomenology, as transcendental philosophy, is the only rigorous science of human experience in that it involves itself with investigating that condition of experience (i.e., consciousness) which alone makes experience and all methods for investigating experience possibilities.

Summarizing the discussion to here: While Kant, Hegel, Kierkegaard, and Husserl approached the concept of transcendental from different perspectives, their understanding of the concept itself is similar. Each philosopher conceived the concept as something that precedes experience a priori, something that makes knowledge of experience possible. With the emergence of Heidegger's philosophy, the tradition of transcendental philosophy experiences a creative synthesis wherein the divergent views of Kant, Hegel, Kierkegaard, and Husserl are reconciled into a perspective that admits a new transcendental claim.

Heidegger's Transcendental Argument

Heidegger's essential project in **Being and Time** was to work out the fundamental question of the meaning of Being. Convinced that the Greeks' initial struggle with this ontological concern created a "dogma" that "trivialized" and "reified"

22. Don Ihde, EXPERIMENTAL PHENOMENOLOGY: An Introduction (G.P. Putnam's Sons, 1977), p. 51.

23. Natanson, Edmund Husserl, PHILOSOPHER OF INFINITE TASKS (Northwestern Univ. Press, 1973), p 6.

both the question and its answer(s), Heidegger sought to rein-
terpret the question by approaching it from a perspective
wherein the question of Being is perforce the most crucial
issue to be resolved. This perspective has its basis in what
Heidegger called "Dasein" (or human being). Heidegger claimed
that only through an investigation of Dasein's existence could
the question be clarified; for Dasein distinguishes itself from
other beings in that it alone is the entity whose own Being
is an issue for itself.[24] To determine its own Being and
thereby approach a clearer understanding of the question,
Heidegger maintained that Dasein must be guided by its own
existence; for "Dasein always understands itself in terms of
its existence--in terms of a possibility of itself. . . . "[25]
With this turn to the lived experience of human being, to
Dasein's "Being-in-the-world," as the primordial level from
which to investigate Being, Heidegger initiated his transcendental argument. This argument can be seen to take form
in Heidegger's appreciation of Kant's transcendental philosophy, Kierkegaard's existentialism as it evolved in his critique
of Hegel, and Husserl's phenomenology.

Specifically, Heidegger saw Kant's argument concerning the
transcendental limits of experience as providing a potential
grounding for what Heidegger called "philosophical anthro-
pology"--the ontological study of man in his everyday existence.[26] However, according to Heidegger, Kant erred in
giving priority to reason and logic as the transcendental
foundations of human experience. The world of human experience always precedes questions of rationality; the world is
"there" before a Kantian "unity of self-consciousness" can
ever arise; that is, "The world is not what I [initially]
think, but what I [initially] live through" as an historical
being.[27] Although the world comes into focus only through
one's conscious acts, it is the world that is presupposed in
any discussion of consciousness. The world and human consciousness therefore are symbiotic: neither can be detached
from the other if either is to be comprehended as meaningful.
For Heidegger, then, this conception of the world must be
acknowledged as "the transcendental background" from which
any ontological investigation of human existence must proceed.[28] Here, Kierkegaard's influence on Heidegger is

24. Heidegger, p. 32.

25. Ibid., p. 33.

26. Heidegger, 38.

27. Maurice Merleau-Ponty, PHENOMENOLGY OF PERCEPTION, tr. Colin Smith
(Routledge & Kegan Paul, 1974), xvi-xvii.

28. Calvin O. Schrag. EXISTENCE AND FREEDOM: Towards an Ontology of Human
Existence (Northwestern Univ. Press, 1970), p. 33.

apparent. For Kierkegaard's critique of Hegel's epistemological pre-judgments concerning "the mind's insight into what knowing is" was reaffirmed by Heidegger. Schrag has clarified this point in the following statement wherein he elucidated a common contention of Kierkegaardian and Heideggerian thought:

> The datum or phenomenon of existence is always prior to any epistemological theories concerning it. That is why epistemology, or the question of knowledge, can never provide a point of departure. It constitutes a secondary and subordinate enquiry. Being precedes knowledge. Knowledge is itself borne and supported by being.[29]

Heidegger chose to investigate the phenomenon of existence by following many of the phenomenological directives offered him by his teacher, Husserl. Specifically, Heidegger argued that only the method of phenomenology teaches us to move toward the "things themselves" in elucidating their nature; only through a phenomenology of existence could a fundamental ontology become possible.[30] But Heidegger did not seek to reduce his analysis of existence to a transcendental ego, for a human being's attachment to the world of experience precludes any such priviledged analytic viewpoint. Paradoxically, Husserl's efforts to establish the certitude of the transcendental ego showed the impossibility of his position; that is, the consciousness of a transcendental ego always attaches it to the world of experience, a world that is not constituted by a transcendental consciousness but makes such a consciousness a possibility. For Heidegger, the meaning of phenomenological description lies not in a transcendental consciousness, but in an "interpretation" (or hermeneutic) of the world as it shows itself through one's everyday existence. "The question of existence never gets straightened out except through existing itself" wherein one's interpretive understanding of the world makes it meaningful.[31]

With Heidegger's hermeneutic adjustment of Husserl's position, "the transcendental descends into history" [32] and becomes the process of interpretive understanding wherein meaning and knowledge originate. To abide by this adjustment of the transcendental required Heidegger to admit the "self-referentiality" of both his argument and his investigative intentions. That is, Heidegger found himself involved in the very conditions of interpretive understanding he sought to

---

29. Ibid., p. 12.

30. Heidegger, p. 60.

31. Heidegger, p. 33.

32. See Maurice Merleau-Ponty, SIGNS, tr. Richard C. McCleary (Northwestern Univ. Press, 1964), p. 107.

demonstrate.[33] But what are these conditions of interpretive understanding from which arises the experiential form of meaning and from which people come to know the world? Only by answering this question could Heidegger substantiate his views concerning the transcendental. He approached this question by investigating the ontological relationship between understanding, interpretation, and meaning. Before examining Heidegger's investigation of this relationship, a point of clarification is needed.

There is perhaps no more difficult requirement for the reader encountering Heidegger for the first time than that of comprehending his ontological description of the "ontical" (i.e., phenomena as they show themselves in the intersubjective world of everyday, common sense existence). The difficulty here occurs when the reader fails to keep in mind that ontological analysis always has its "roots" in the ontical; ontological analysis is directed by the specific ontical phenomenon being investigated. The purpose of ontological analysis is to elucidate the presuppositions of the ontical and, in so doing, to provide the ontical with a "conceptual clarification."[34] This conceptual clarification enables one to **observe** what is typically only **seen** in the world of the ontical. That is, to observe something is to be more descriptive and "systematic" in one's investigation of the something than if one only reports that the something has been seen. A creative illustration of this point is found in a brief dialogue between the famous detective Sherlock Holmes and his faithful companion Dr. Watson wherein Holmes explains how the power of observation produced his incredible feats of deduction:

> "You see, but you do not observe," remarked Holmes to Watson. "The distinction is clear. For example, you have frequently seen the steps which lead up from the hall to this room."
>
> "Frequently."
>
> "How often?"
>
> "Well, some hundreds of times."
>
> "Then how many are there?"
>
> "How many! I don't know."
>
> "Quite so! You have not observed. And yet you have seen. That is just my point. Now, I know that there are seventeen steps, because I have both seen and observed."[35]

33. Cf. Rüdiger Bubner, "Is Transcendental Hermeneutics Possible?" in ESSAYS ON EXPLANATION AND UNDERSTANDING, ed. Juha Manninen and Raimo Tuomela (D. Reidel, 1976), pp. 59–77.

34. See Heidegger, p. 34; also Schrag, EXISTENCE AND FREEDOM, p. 32.

35. Arthur Conan Doyle, "A Scandal in Bohemia," in THE COMPLETE ORIGINAL ILLUSTRATED SHERLOCK HOLMES (Castle Books, 1976), pp. 12–13.

Hence, what Watson saw as steps can be defined more carefully by observing (describing) how these particular steps
exist and thereby function to aid those who care to visit
Holmes in his room. A description of the steps not only would
show that they are seventeen in number, but also that they
possibly ascend at a thirty-five degree angle, that they are
made of wood, that they purposively squeak to warn Holmes
of visitors, and so on. All of these descriptive features make
up the "what" of the object that Watson has seen "some hun-
dreds of times"; they constitute the steps' eidetic features
which enable the steps to serve their function and which
enable people like Watson to identify them as steps. In other
words, what the steps are is a function of how they exist.
Yet, in the world of the ontical, of everyday common sense,
designating what the steps are does not usually include an
awareness of, or an explicit descriptive statement about, how
they exist. Common sense is content with the tautological
claim that "steps are steps." Common sense too often takes
for granted the "how" and thus obscures a precise description
of the "what."

When Heidegger spoke of understanding, interpretation, and
meaning—phenomena that have been talked about "some hun-
dreds of times"—he did so ontologically. That is, he observed
these phenomena in their ontical state and then described
their presuppositions, their essences. Hence, Heidegger was
concerned with showing **how** everyday understanding, interpretation, and meaning originate in the world of intersubjectivity, of common sense.

The ontological relationship between understanding, interpretation, and meaning is founded in what Heidegger designated
as **Logos**—the language of Being—or what his student,
Gadamer, designated as the "universality of human linguisticality."[36] Both of these designations point to an ontological
conception of language, a conception that correlates language
with Dasein's experiential existence. Conceived this way,
language becomes more than an ontical phenomenon, that is,
a tool or object for manipulating experience; it also assumes
a primordial character thereby becoming the "horizon" which
gives background to all possible experiences. As Gadamer
pointed out, ". . . language is not only an object in our
hands, it is the reservoir of tradition and the medium in
and through which we exist and perceive our world."[37]
Here it is reasonable to ask: Is there any thing beyond the
horizon of language which makes a knowledge of the world

36. Hans-Georg Gadamer, PHILOSOPHICAL HERMENEUTICS, tr. and ed. David
E. Linge (University of California Press, 1976), p. 25.

37. Ibid., p. 29.

portance of Heidegger's argument lies in its ackno
nt of the limitation, its ability to make explicit t
ns that give force to the limitation, and its challen
eged alternative perspectives that such conditio
tely may not be forfeited if the general claim
ige is to remain meaningful."[46]

Implications

er's transcendental argument offers an importa
re to communication researchers, one that clear
the traditional scientific approach advocated by mai
nt researchers in the field. While Heidegger, througho
itings, suggested this directive, Merleau-Ponty's form
is most appropriate for the purposes here:

All my knowledge of the world, even my scientific knowledge,
is gained from my own particular point of view, or from
some experience of the world without which the symbols of
science would be meaningless. The whole universe of science
is built upon the world as directly experienced, and if we
want to subject science itself to rigorous scrutiny and arrive
at a precise assessment of its meaning and scope, we must
begin by reawakening the basic experience of the world of
which science is the second-order expression. Science has
not and never will have, by its nature, the same significance
qua form of being as the world which we perceive, for the
simple reason that it is a rationale or explanation of that
world. . . . To return to things themselves is to return
to that world which precedes knowledge, of which knowledge
always speaks, and in relation to which every scientific
schematization is an abstract and derivative sign-language,
as is geography in relation to the countryside in which we
have learnt beforehand what a forest, a prairie or a river
is.[47]

Merleau-Ponty is echoing Heidegger's claim about th
ndental ground of all human experience--the ontologica
nship between understanding, interpretation, an
g. Science is only one mode of understanding wherei
ld-view is created through an act of interpretation-
cific abstracting and structuring of language tha
s the world in a meaningful, but biasd, way. Thi
s not bad, it is inevitable; for all human beings ar
ned to bias as long as they must construct vision
world by making choices from the universe of linguisti
lities. While the communication scientist may acknowl
he bias, Heidegger, by "returning to the world" fro
the bias originates, attempted to observe and clarif
nesis. In so doing, Heidegger established a hermeneuti

Bubner, p. 71.

Merleau-Ponty, THE PHENOMENOLOGY OF PERCEPTION, pp. viii-ix.

possible? Perhaps, but for a finite human being, the question avoids any answer more definite than, say, Kierkegaard's "leap of faith" or Wittgenstein's silence.[38] Hence, the injunction that language imposes against human beings and, in so doing, grants itself a primordial status, is this: "We cannot see a linguistic world from above . . . for there is no point of view outside the experience of the world in language which it could itself become an object."[39]

Accepting that all experiential existence is a language phenomenon, Heidegger set out to show how this phenomenon presents itself to human beings. Here he elucidated the ontological relationship between understanding, interpretation, and meaning; for Heidegger maintained that this relationship describes the process of human linguisticality as it unfolds existentially. It is in this unfolding of language, according to Heidegger, that Being is revealed (**aletheia**); or as Gadamer phrased it: "Being that can be understood is language."[40]

As understanding, language is the universe of linguistic possibilities that is revealed both **in** and **through** time. While Heidegger acknowledged these two dimensions of linguistic temporality in his discussion of what he called Dasein's "hermeneutical situation," a more specific designation of these dimensions, which is consistent with Heidegger's approach, is provided by those phenomenologists who have appropriated the linguists' distinction of "synchrony" and "diachrony" for designating, respectively, languages' in and through temporal structure.[41] Simply stated, language as understanding is synchronic as it shows itself in a specific culture's use of language; language as understanding is diachronic as it shows itself through its historical movement, through the possible changes it undergoes from time past, to time present, and time future.

In Heidegger's discussion of understanding, he gave priority to this diachronic movement, or what he called the "projective character" of understanding. Understanding is projective because in its historical movement toward the future, it not only reveals the language of Being as something that was or is, but also as something that can be. This "potentiality" of language as understanding is crucial to Heidegger's existential analytic of Dasein; for Heidegger's correlation of language with Dasein's experiential existence leads to the

38. Ludwig Wittgenstein, TRACTATUS LOGICO-PHILOSOPHICUS (Humanities Press, 1951), p. 189.

39. Gadamer, TRUTH AND METHOD, p. 410.

40. Ibid., p. 432.

41. See, for example, Ricoeur, pp. 27-96.

conclusion that Dasein's own Being is itself understanding. As understanding, Dasein is that Being who is guided not only by its past and its present concerns, but also by its futural development--what it can become. **"Understanding is the existential Being of Dasein's own potentiality-for-Being; and it is so in such a way that this Being discloses in itself what its Being is capable of."[42]**

When Heidegger observed how understanding is "made-known" to individuals on both an intrapersonal and interpersonal level, his analysis turned to the synchronic dimension of language. Here he showed how understanding is related specifically to interpretation and meaning. Within any given culture, understanding is the realm of linguistic possibilities that constitutes the culture's **Weltanschauung,** its intersubjective world-view that delineates the culture's present limits of rationality. Emphasizing that a culture's understanding is "in advance" of, and thereby makes possible, any particular act of interpretive understanding, Heidegger designated this ontological realm of understanding, a "fore-having." A culture's fore-having is its linguistic horizon that forms the context for the culture's patterns of thought and behavior.

The development of understanding within a particular culture (or through history is general) is "interpretation." According to Heidegger,

> In interpretation, understanding does not become something different. It becomes itself. Such interpretation is guided existentially in understanding; the latter does not arise from the former. Nor is interpretation the acquiring of information about what is understood; it is rather the working-out of possibilities projected in understanding.[43]

(Here, again, one sees Heidegger's acknowledgement of Dasein's linguistic constraints, beyond which an understanding of Being is incomprehensible.) This working-out of linguistic possibilities is itself contingent on how a culture's members **appropriate** and **conceptualize** the possibilities (fore-having) "in advance" of any concrete act of interpretive understanding. The appropriation of a culture's fore-having originates what Heidegger labeled the "fore-sight" of the culture's members. An individual's fore-sight is those linguistic possibilities that the individual has appropriated from his/her fore-having and which constitute the particular "points of views" that fix "that with regard to which what is understood is to be interpreted."[44] The often discussed phenomenon of "selective

42. Heidegger, p. 184.

43. Ibid., pp. 188-189.

44. Ibid., p. 191.

perception" is an ontic presentation of designated ontologically as a point of of understanding. Understanding is dev linguistic possibilities of an individual' ceptualized by the individual into s thought for the purposes of conceiving ways. Since this conceptualization prece of interpretive understanding, Heidegge a person's "fore-conception." Communica following the work of George Kelly, discus in terms of an individual's system of are essentially rediscovering and operat formulations about the fore-conception of u

According to Heidegger, once a particula is interpreted in terms of a person's that the "intelligibility" of the object person, the object becomes meaningful. "meaning" to the above discussion of und pretation is made clear by Heidegger in tion:

> When entities within-the-world . . . have stood--we say that they have **meaning.** . is understood, taken strictly, is not th entity, or alternatively, Being. Meanin the intelligibility . . . of something ma which can be Articulated in a disclosure stand, we call "meaning." The **concept** the formal existential framework of what to that which an understanding interpr **Meaning is the "upon which" of a pro which something becomes intelligible as its structure from a fore-having, a fore- conception.**[45]

Admittedly, the above discussion of He analytic of human understanding, interpr is a simplification of what, in his described methodically as the transcen human experience from which the possi arise. What must be remembered here Heidegger's analysis offers, at best, an tation of these conditions; that is, Hei to the limitation imposed by language, underlies his transcendental argument. B ment suggests that this limitation is one spective employed for investigating the hur

45. Heidegger, pp. 192-193. Also see Michael J. Hyde meneutics and Rhetoric: A Seen But Unobserved Relatior OF SPEECH 65 (1979), 347-63.

the in ledgem condit to a "ultim knowle

Heideg direct affect promi his w lation

Here trans relat mean a we a s exhit bias cond of th possi edge whic its directive that questions science's tendency to assert "episte-mological first principles." Science comes to know the world, not vice versa. It is in this coming to know the world that one acquires, to borrow an expression from Noam Chomsky, a "linguistic competence" which serves to order the world. Thus, when scientists make their linguistic competence the criterion of the world's truth, they obscure the transcendental ground which makes their competence a possibility; they "sever the phenomena from the method."

Admittedly, there exists a passivity in Heidegger's transcen-dental argument, a passivity that shows itself in the argu-ment's "dogmatic" allegiance to language. Can science respond to this passivity even though scientific reflection is itself a linguistic act and thereby an affirmation of Heidegger's argument? An answer to this question--as it pertains specifi-cally to communication research--is offered by both Habermas and Apel.

Habermas has argued that the transcendental claim of Heidegger's argument is insufficient for comprehending how language, through the practice of speech, constitutes histori-cal existence.[48] According to Habermas, by absolutizing language as the "reservoir" of experiential existence, one fails to appreciate not only how the practice of speech can be used in a distortive way, but also how critical (scientific) reflection can remedy such distortions by producing a "con-ceptual system" for conducting "rational" discourse. Habermas's research program (termed "universal pragmatics") is directed toward this goal: a "reconstructing" of "the universal validity basis of speech," a basis which can be used as a dialogical tool for scientific reflection when investigating the practice of speech in communication interactions.[49]

Unfortunately, Habermas's zeal to dissociate his scientific research program from transcendental philosophy has confused the fact that his program affirms Heidegger's transcendental argument.[50] That is, if Habermas can substantiate scientifi-cally how a dialogue "ought to be" performed to meet the conditions of rationality underlying dialogue, then he would produce, at best, a language-game (in Wittgenstein's sense of the term) for guiding the process of "understanding-interpretation-meaning." The adequacy of this language-game, however, would always have to answer to the process from which it is drawn.

48. See his ZUR LOGIK DER SOZIALWISSENSCHAFTEN (Suhrkamp, 1970).

49. See "What is Universal Pragmatics?" in his COMMUNICATION AND THE EVOL-UTION OF SOCIETY, tr. Thomas McCarthy (Beacon, 1979), pp. 1-68.

50. See Habermas, "What is Universal Pragmatics," esp. pp. 21-25.

Unlike Habermas, Apel has not been mislead by the "insufficiency" of Heidegger's transcendental argument; rather, he has clarified the insufficiency in terms of the argument. In Apel's view, Heidegger's argument correctly suggests "that the life-world has always been interpreted linguistically and that the **a priori** of communicating in everyday language within the context of the life-world is, in a precisely definable sense, the irreducible precondition for the possibility and intersubjective validity of all conceivable philosophical or scientific theory-formation and even of the 'reconstruction' . . . of language itself."[51] The insufficiency of this thesis, according to Apel, is that it fails to account for the role of argumentation in the construction of knowledge and, as a result, does not suggest a standard from which the logical validity of arguments can be tested to determine their ethical and moral consequences.[52] Clearly, Apel's position here parallels Habermas's critique. But Apel, unlike Habermas, has a much better sense of the presuppositions which make possible his proposal. For as he has noted,

> The logical validity of arguments cannot be tested without, in principle, positing a community of scholars who are capable of both intersubjective communication and reaching a consensus. Even the **de facto** solitary scholar can only explicate and test his line of argument in so far as he is able to internalize the dialogue of a potential community of argumentation in the critical "discourse of the soul with itself". . . . This proves that the **validity** of solitary thought is basically dependent upon the justification of verbal arguments in the actual community of argumentation.[53]

By making the rhetorical practice of argumentation—as such practice is made possible by the intersubjectivity of a "communication community"—the primary concern of transcendental philosophy, Apel has accommodated the views of both Heidegger and Habermas: The process of "understanding-interpretation-meaning" must now seek directives from science's argumentative appeal to "the logically correct use of intellect"; science, however, must recognize that its appeal is a rhetorically-oriented communicative act, one that occurs in the concrete, **but developing,** historical situation of a communication community. Here, confronted by the "moral norms of the communication community," the logically correct use of intellect necessarily finds its limitations in what Apel has described as the "**a priori** of argumentation":

51. Karl-Otto Apel, "The Communication Community and the Foundations of Ethics," in his TOWARDS A TRANSFORMATION OF PHILOSOPHY, p. 251.

52. Due to this insufficiency, Apel has labeled Heidegger's argument "quasi-transcendental."

53. Apel, p. 258.

> Anyone who takes part in an argument implicitly acknowledges all the **potential claims** of all the members of the communication community that **can** be justified [sic] by rational arguments (otherwise the claim of argumentation would restrict itself in subject matter). He also commits himself to eventually justifying all his claims upon other people through arguments. Furthermore, . . . the members of the communication community (and this implies all thinking beings) are also committed to considering all the potential claims of all the potential members—and this means all human "needs" inasmuch as they could be affected by norms and consequently make **claims** on their fellow human beings. As potential "claims" that can be communicated interpersonally, all human "needs" are ethically **relevant**. They must be **acknowledged** if they can be justified interpersonally through arguments.[54]

The "reflexive" moment of scientific inquiry occurs as science recognizes its ethical commitment to its presuppositions: the **a priori** of argumentation and the moral norms of the communication community. Disregarding such reflexivity, and appealing only to the logically correct use of intellect, science dramatizes "the very present danger of a technocracy."[55]

Conclusion

To appreciate the role played by the transcendental in human communication is to find both a directive and an inspiration for doing communication research. The directive, as suggested in this paper, is found in what the "demand for reflexivity" entails;[56] the inspiration is echoed in this demand as the demand has taken form in the philosophies of those such as Heidegger, Habermas, and Apel. That is, in Habermas's and Apel's extensions of Heidegger's transcendental argument, one hears not only an affirmation of communication research, but also a call for the necessity of such research. Concerning this later point, Schrag's critique of Apel's transcendental philosophy of argumentation is suggestive. According to Schrag, Apel has failed to recognize that "argumentative competence" is not a precondition for the uses of language in, for example, "gestural signification," "performative utterances," and

54. Ibid., p. 277.

55. Karl-Otto Apel, "The A Priori of Communication and the Foundation of the Humanities," MAN AND WORLD, 5(1972), 28. For a discussion of how this "danger" is typified in Habermas's research program, see John O'Neill, "Critique and Remembrance," in ON CRITICAL THEORY, ed. John O'Neill (Seabury, 1976), pp. 1-11.

56. For examples of communication research that respond to this "demand," see Joseph J. Pilotta, "Presentational Thinking: A Contemporary Hermeneutic of Communicative Action," WESTERN JOURNAL OF SPEECH COMMUNICATION, 4 (1979), 288-300; also see my "The Experience of Anxiety: A Phenomenological Investigation," QUARTERLY JOURNAL OF SPEECH, 66 (1980), 140-54; and my "Philosophical Hermeneutics and the Communicative Experience: The Paradigm of Oral History," MAN AND WORLD, 13 (1980), 81-98.

"mytho-poetic disclosure."[57] That such uses of language have received, and continue to receive, much attention by communication scholars, suggests the potential contributions which these scholars can offer as they consider the role of the transcendental in human communication.

57. Schrag, RADICAL REFLECTION AND THE ORIGIN OF THE HUMAN SCIENCES, p. 23.

Communicative Competence as a Research Criterion: A Philosophy of Social Science Directive

Joseph J. Pilotta

Part One

The intention of this essay is to present a logic of social science based on communicative competence which is the condition for concrete mutual interaction.

Such a criterion is necessary given the recent literature regarding the field's quest for self-identity, and the socially unaware advocacies to "keep the faith" in the Faustian science of results.[1] The philosophers of science, e.g. Hanson [2] and Toulmin,[3] have established that the justification for science in general is recourse to a speech community's rule based consensus. But the social sciences are a special case, for it is my contention that the social sciences in principle must be capable of being used by objects (possible subjects) for their own self-understanding. Thus communication theory as a social science must in order to justify itself be comprised by more than a community of scientists. A hypothesis cannot be corroborated or falsified with recourse to "pure" observation of scientists (subjects) upon objects. But, the objects of social

INTERPERSONAL COMMUNICATION: Essays in Phenomenology and Hermeneutics, ed., Joseph J. Pilotta, Copyright 1982, The Center for Advanced Research in Phenomenology, Inc. and co-published by arrangement with The University Press of America, Inc.

1. G.R. Miller and C.R. Berger, "On Keeping the Faith in Matters Scientific," WESTERN JOURNAL OF SPEECH COMMUNICATION, 1978, 42, pp. 44-57. It is my concern that statements of this kind may be taken at face-value and used as justification to be self-exempt from social concerns. Let us hope that a Project Camelot is not in the future for the field of communication. See I.L. Horowitz, (Ed.), THE RISE AND FALL OF PROJECT CAMELOT: Studies in the Relationship Between Social Science and Practical Politics (MIT Press, 1967); also, W.B. Littrell and G. Sjoberg (Eds.), CURRENT ISSUES IN SOCIAL POLICY (Sage, 1976).

2. N.R. Hanson, PATTERNS OF DISCOVERY: An Inquiry Into the Conceptual Foundations of Science (Cambridge University, 1958).

3. S. Toulmin, THE PHILOSOPHY OF SCIENCE: An Introduction (Cambridge University, 1968).

science are co-subjects of the social scientist who are of interest. The co-subject is not merely of interest as an entity whose behavior is to be observed and explained, but primarily as a partner in communication with each other. Therefore, social science fundamentally entails the understanding of intended meaning.

If the justification of science in general is a recourse to a speech community and this means that rules (norms) can be followed and reflected upon among students, then social science, given that their objects are co-subjects, must incorporate their objects into their speech community. Therefore, the social scientist operates in a participatory or a mutual interaction community. The social scientific community criterion in order to reach consensus must incorporate society as the subject-object of its science. Social science and the field of communication needs to justify itself on the basis of a speech community logic in which: (a) the scientist is participant as well as observer, (b) the object of communication investigation is also a co-subject.

To accomplish this task, I will discuss:

(1) the communication competence model as the condition for mutual interaction;

(2) the structure of complementarity or synchronization as a requirement of interpersonal competence;

(3) the reflection process upon the structure of interpersonal competence reveals an atemporal or invariant structure of meaning and atemporal dimension of historical mediation; and

(4) the structure of the transcendental (the conditions for any awareness) and tradition-mediation (hermeneutics) are requirements for communicative competence as a three-valued social research logic.

Communicative Competence and Synchrony

Communicative competence has been defined by Wiemann as:

> The ability of an interactant to choose among available communicative behaviors in order that he may successfully accomplish his own interpersonal goals during an encounter while maintaining the face and line of his fellow interactants, within the constraints of the situation.[4]

4. J.M. Wiemann, "Explication and Test of a Model of Communicative Competence," HUMAN COMMUNICATION RESEARCH, 1977, 3, p. 198.

Researchers have identified consistently three dimensions of communicative competence:

> . . . (1) Empathy, (2) behavioral flexibility that is, the ability to choose the most appropriate role for oneself to play from among all available roles in one's repertory; and (3) interaction management--the skill needed to carry off the procedural aspects of a conversation in a satisfying way, e.g., not interrupting a conversation partner.[5]

The argument advanced by the advocates of communicative competence research in our field is summarized aptly by Brandt:

> . . . Proponents of the communicative competence position maintain that in order for persons to achieve social goals through communication, they must learn to enact behavioral routines which are deemed appropriate to the particular individuals and social situations where they are inter-acting.[6]

If we look across these elements of competence we find the-oretical significance **qua** philosophy of science. The key terms **appropriate** and **interaction** emphasize an other-orientation based on social acceptability. This means that rules are not formed in isolation but are to be based on the condition of commonality which can be followed and reflected upon. Com-municative competence also emphasizes the flexibililty to choose a role appropriately. This emphasizes a self-reflexive capacity as well as a quality that we term empathic. Empathy **qua** philosophy of science is the attempt to "fill in" the subject-object gap. Empathy is a "filler" because it is a part of the neo-positivist tradition which still treats the co-subject as an object. Communicative competence focuses upon the anthropological capacities of being able to learn the appro-priate conduct of a community. This means that anthropologi-cally, communicative competence as a strategy has as its goal "survival of the species": mutual (cooperative) inter-action. Therefore, social appropriateness reveals an intimate involvement and a synchrony which establishes intersub-jectivity, but belongs to neither subject.[7]

Merleau-Ponty summarizes communicative competence as a form of intersubjective behavior by pointing out that speaking

5. J.M. Wiemann, "Needed Research and Training in Speaking and Listening Literacy," COMMUNICATION EDUCATION, 1978, 27, p. 313.

6. D.R. Brandt, "On Linking Social Performance with Social Competence: Some Relations Between Communicative Style and Attributions of Interpersonal Attrac-tiveness and Effectiveness," HUMAN COMMUNICATION RESEARCH, 1979, 5, p. 224.

7. D.J. Cegala, "Interaction Involvement: A Cognitive Dimension of Communi-cative Competence," COMMUNICATION EDUCATION, 1981, 30.

subjects project through words a meaning which we apprehend bodily as an intention which our lived bodies assume:

> . . . Taking up another's intention is not thinking on my own part, but a synchronizing of my existence, a transformation of my own being.[8]

Thinking, and also speech, are already intersubjective in the sense that it is bodily intentionality operative in a structure of behavior:

> The phonetic gesture brings about for both the speaking subject and his hearers, a certain structural coordination of experience, a certain modulation of existence; exactly as a pattern of my bodily behavior endows objects around me with a certain significance, for me and for others.[9]

The social psychologist Ragnar Rommetveit characterized the structure of synchrony in terms of a complementarity of encoding and decoding:

> The full fledged act of verbal communication is thus under normal conditions based upon a reciprocally endorsed spontaneously fulfilled contract of complementarity: **encoding** is tacitly assumed to involve **anticipatory decoding,** i.e., it is taken for granted that speech is continuously listener-oriented and monitored in accordance with assumptions concerning a **shared** social world and convergent strategies of categorization. Conversely--and on precisely those premises--**decoding** is tacitly assumed to be speaker-oriented and aiming at **a reconstruction of what the speaker intends to make known.**[10]

Rommetveit points out that anticipation is a shared temporality and the distinction between encoding and decoding are not mutually exclusive acts but are simultaneous processes.

The importance of the encoding-decoding complementarity is that it disrupts the dualism of self and other as an object of purpose, aims and affectivities. It also disallows the rubric of objectivity and subjectivity constituted by the traditional subject-object dichotomy. The structure of complementarity reveals a "commonness" or shared temporality as well as a monitoring process. The monitoring process is constituted by a common meaning. The common meaning constitutes the **reiterable** and atemporality of meaning which endures across temporally variant dimensions. This invariant structure of

---

8. M. Merleau-Ponty, PHENOMENOLOGY OF PERCEPTION, trans. Collin Smith (Humanities Press, Inc., 1962), p. 184.

9. Ibid., p. 193.

10. R. Rommetveit, ON MESSAGE STRUCTURE (John Wiley & Sons, 1974), p. 55.

meaning is characterized as accessible to all inasmuch as
it is constituted through mutual interaction. The relationship
of meaning (invariant) and synchrony has relevance for cultural linguistics.

We realize that the project of communicative competence has
developed in the tradition of cultural linguistics and generally
has been based on the pragmatic-behavioral paradigm.[11]
As Paulson says:

> Since the publication of Gumperz and Hymes, "The Ethnogra-
> phy of Communication" in 1969, a great many social linguists
> have been trying to discover and understand the rules of
> speaking which underlie utterances and invest them with
> social meaning. Communicative competence is not simply a
> term: it is a concept basic to understanding social inter-
> action.[12]

Hence, the interaction of linguistics and meaning within the
communicative competence paradigm assumes that every utterance demands an **appropriate integration into a context.**

Thus, any particular element of a culture refers inevitably
to a whole which establishes the meaning of those elements.
There is a reciprocal relationship of understanding obtained
between a particular feature and the whole of which it is
a feature. The expression, while transparent with the meaning
must, at the same time co-imply other expressions thus composing a matrix of inter-connected meanings revealing at their
fundamental level the manner in which the significance comprises a unitary world. Each expression, while manifesting
the basic cultural outline, implicates as well other expressions revealing the same cultural matrix. One significance
reveals all significances and cannot be completely understood
without them, while all significances are implicitly present
in one significance. **This is the basis for the understanding
of cultural linguistics as well as communicative competence.**
A word spoken in a sentence does not gain its sense only
from the relationships of the words within a sentence, rather
the sense also arises within a system of a total linguistic
field carried by "tradition" and present to the speaker and
hearer. Each sentence implicates the entire language and
the entire language is manifest in each sentence. The entire
linguistic field and all that it signifies must be present if
the specific words and sentences are to be understood, and
they will be understood to the extent that the linguistic

11. J.M. Wiemann, "Needed Research and Training in Speaking and Listening
Literacy."

12. C.B. Paulson, "Linguistic and Communicative Competence," TESOL QUARTERLY,
1974, 8, p. 349.

field is present. **This is the cultural basis for "communicative competence."**

Benjamin Whorf has offered the thesis that a "grammar" of culture is reflected in and shaped by the linguistic structures of a particular group. The "power" of the word cannot be contested. In various cultures it was invested with the divine power of creation itself. Any investigation of a particular cultural world necessitates the investigation of the "grammar" of a language used in that culture. Yet, while the logical and grammatico-structural approaches give us the coherent relationships among terms and their usages and their designations, they assume that language expresses solely such relationships and designations. Indeed, such designations include not only things but also ideas, images, beliefs, values and other intangible aspects of the particular cultural world. Yet, language is more than that.

While indicating things and topics, language also manifests the structuration of experiences and perceptions which have a "life of their own." Language reveals that while states-of-affairs can remain the same, the experience of them may change. Conversely, although empirical conditions may change, the experience of them, articulated in language, may remain constant. This noncoincidence between language and the empirical, between experience and the empirical, suggests that there is a complementarity between language and experience.

Language plays a crucial role in experience; its grammar does not always coincide with the experiential process. There is a variation between experience and linguistic habits. This means that language may remain constant while the experience has changed or conversely, experience may remain constant while language shifts. This also can be said with respect to things, as noted above. Hence what a propositional language cannot express, poetic language may convey, dance may reveal or art works make visible. All these factors must be accepted under the notion of "linguistic understanding."

Language has a "dialogical medium."[13] This means that the individual in this medium is shaped and shapes others. The individual's perceptions and those of others are mutually shaped in linguistic interaction. At the level of linguistic interaction, the dialogical medium is equivalent to the structure of complementarity which occurs at many levels. Non-verbal gestures and eye gaze are instances of mutual

---

13. See Algis Mickunas, "The Dialogical Region," in this volume.

interaction.[14] Moreover, interaction dimensions include the linguistic significations of past generations embodied in styles of writing, monument inscriptions, sayings and stories. Hence, language is to be understood in its broadest sense to include any expression. Language, therefore, presupposes the whole of a socio-history (temporality) and reveals itself as competent through an atemporality given to itself.

The model of mutual interaction based on common meaning (invariance) and mediated by the tradition of a particular speech community provides a model of communicative competence as a criterion for social research. The model proposed incorporates the complementarity of the transcendental region of phenomenology and the hermeneutical orientation.

Part Two

It is appropriate at this point to offer a definitional clarification of fundamental terms employed in this paper.

Hermeneutics is human self-understanding based upon the embedded tradition of a speech community.

Phenomenology is the science of meaning-structures (**eidos**) which are accessible to anyone, at any time.

Transcendental is the region of meaning which is an invariant, atemporal structure. (The atemporal is used in the Greek sense of **alpha-privativum** which is an intensification of time rather than a negative-prefix which signifies a deprivation of temporality.)

The Law of Contradiction and Its Limit [15]

Phenomenology emerged in the late nineteenth century within the controversy concerning the foundations of science and logic. The explanatory power of the method of the physical sciences had assumed such a dominance that the physical sciences found themselves in the position to make claims of being the basis of all objective knowledge. Any endeavor, desiring to assume the name of science, was compelled to assume that the basis of all knowledge must lie in the empirical-naturalistic or physicalistic approach. Following this lead, sciences such as psychology advanced the notion that since logic is fundamental to scientific work, it too should be based on empirically observable and describable facts.

14. D.J. Cegala, S. Sokuvitz, and A.F. Alexander, "An Investigation of Eye Gaze and Its Relation to Selected Verbal Behavior," HUMAN COMMUNICATION RESEARCH, 1979, 5, pp. 99-108.

15. The development of this discussion is in A. Mickunas and J. Pilotta, booklength manuscript, THE PHENOMENOLOGICAL SCIENCE OF COMMUNICATION (unpublished).

The claim was human beings use logic in their scientific theories, therefore logic should be based on the empirically observable functions of human beings. Psychology, being the empirical study of human mind and its scientifically decipherable laws, should assume the burden of being the foundational science of logic. By implication this also meant that psychology should be the basis of all sciences, inasmuch as all sciences employ logical procedures in their theoretical work.

This proposed foundation means that the laws of logic and even mathematics consist of generalizations of empirically observable psychological phenomena or facts. We know that people can count, therefore numbers can be derived from the fact of counting. We know that people see empirically one color at one time and not two. Therefore we can derive the notion that one thing cannot be blue and red at the same time. If we generalize this notion from the various observations of our empirical experience, we can derive the principle of non-contradiction: it is false to say that the same thing can have two opposing characteristics at the same time and in the same respect. This view can be completed by adding the concepts of association and causality. The present blue color of a thing reminds me of, or is associated with, the previous experiences of blue and not red leading to the notion that past experience is a corrective for the present and the present for the past. This view is guaranteed by the notion of causality. The things and their properties leave or cause impressions in the human experiencer. Hence the blue color causes one to see blue and not red, which allows one to correct experiences by rechecking the source of the impression. I thought I saw red, but actually the thing is blue. Therefore, the principle of contradiction is derived from empirical observation.

This relationship of logical process to empirical phenomena seems to be tenuous. For instance, when a mathematician deals with negative numbers, there are **no** empirical phenomena to correlate or even a memory of an empirical phenomenon which correlates to a negative number. Hence, the logic of mathematics does not rest on empirical-psychological observation.

It appears as well that the logic of meaning in the communicative event is not based on the empirical-psychological either. The reasons are:

(1) When we make a statement "The storm is furious" we may vary the sounds empirically, we may say it in German, Chinese or French without changing the meaning of the statement. We may say it slowly, rapidly or we may stutter, but

across these variations the meaning remains constant. The meaning is distinct from the empirical modalities of its expression.

(2) In the process of making the statement we may have various changing psychological attitudes: we may be elated, afraid, indifferent, we may perform psychological associations with previously experienced storms in which we were terrified; yet these psychological variations do not change the meaning of the statement. It remains constant.

(3) Even if in our vocal expressions the psychological attitudes are manifest, such as when one voices the statement indifferently, exuberantly, etc., one does not change the meaning of the statement. We merely reveal our psychological relationship to the storm. What is primarily communicated is meaning whose understanding is required for the understanding of the psychological states expressed through empirical sounds or gestures.

Therefore, the logic of meaning is not derivable from the empirical, but is a logic that is **invariant**. This meaning-logic testifies to the expression "we can say the same thing in different ways." Therefore, expression based on meaning-logic is never contradictory even if the expression is empirically varied.

The Canons of Scientific Logic in Question

Most recently within the sciences, the fundamental canons of science, the law of non-contradiction and the law of the excluded-middle have been put into question. In the field of physics mutual recognition of particle and wave, as delineated through the Bohr-Helsenberg formulation, demands a logic outside of the traditional two-valued logic.[16] This means that the logic of science has a rational exclusivity, i.e., light **either** appears as a wave **or** as a particle is not an admissible scientific statement. When the subject-object dichotomy is maintained in communication research, it leads to inherent difficulties.

> The attempt to account for conversational sequences as persons switch partners is really nothing more than the question of how to get dyads from individuals. I take this question to be a fundamental question in any theory of two-person

16. J. Gebser, VERFALL AND TEILHABE: Uber Polarität, Dualität, Identität und den Ursprung (Stuttgart, 1977).

> interaction. It is a simple matter to characterize individual
> or dyadic interaction alone, but it is no small matter to
> describe how dyadic interaction processes derive from the
> styles of the individuals who make up the dyad.[17]

Eradication of this dualistic logic means that the dichotomy
of subject:object is philosophically untenable. The manifestation of light as a particle/wave means that particle/wave
continuously and mutually explicate the phenomena. The mutual
explication of phenomena is a complementarity. Complementarity introduces the principle of "indeterminacy" into our
scientific logic. Indeterminacy methodologically means the
world is inseparable from the view of the subject.

The European social thinker and philosopher of science, Karl-
Otto Apel has made an appeal to the social science community
that complementarity is a condition of the social science.
This declaration by Apel is based on Karl Popper's attempt
to find observational and falsification propositions.[18] It
has been concluded by Apel that these propositions can only
be decided by the rule within a scientific community. But
these rules are not a part of the scientific theory or the
observational propositions. Therefore, empirical social science
whose objective is the social explanation of facts demands
an interpretive-community as a criterion for success. Explanation and interpretation are not opposites but complementary.

Two-valued logic as the governing principle of cross-cultural
studies has been cited as a logic which occludes our investigations. In the article "Mass Media and Politics," Ithiel De
Sola Pool comes to this conclusion:

> To evaluate assertions primarily by a criterion of objective
> truth is not a natural way of doing things; it is one of
> the peculiar features of the Graeco-Roman-Western tradition.
> This one cultural heritage among the many in human experi-
> ence has tended to make truth-value the main test of the
> validity of statements. And truth-value is a curious criterion.
> It is ruthlessly two-valued and dominated by the excluded
> middle, something which classical Indian logic, for example,
> never accepted; statement in the latter system could be simul-
> taneously both true and false. . . . Western criteria of
> truth assumes further that validity can be tested indepen-
> dently of those doing the testing provided that certain rituals
> of procedures are followed.[19]

17. J.N. Cappella, "Talk and Silence Sequences in Informal Conversations"
II, HUMAN COMMUNICATION RESEARCH, 1980, 6, pp. 130-145.

18. K. Popper, THE LOGIC OF SCIENTIFIC DISCOVERY (Hutchinson, 1959).

19. I.D. Pool, "The Mass Media and Politics in the Modernization Process,"
in L. Pye (Ed.), COMMUNICATIONS AND POLITICAL DEVELOPMENT (Princeton
University Press, 1963), p. 242.

Similarly, in a colloquim, Douglas Ehninger pointed out the limitation of the two-valued logic of "either-or" and that rhetoric has to assume a different logic.[20]

Briefly, two-valued logic assumes (a) a definite point of view, and (b) a direct and unambiguous premise which proceeds to the object of contemplation. In this logic, two opposite statements cannot be true at the same time, thus there belongs no third possibility (**tertium non datur**). This is the famous principle of non-contradiction. The two values are:

    1. Being; the existence of the object

    2. Non-being

But as previously pointed, two-valued logic is suspect, limited and culturally bound. Some have pointed out that another logic is required, as in the case of the Bohr-Heisenberg thesis. Today, in communication research we have accepted the metaphors of "openness," "indeterminacy," "possibility," and "wholeness" as differentiated from potentiality and "qualitative" as desirable characteristics for the accomplishment of communication science. All of these terms suggest a **power** that has been hidden within the dominion of the two-valued system. These metaphors have become part of our communication/ community. The aforementioned twentieth century accomplishments in the field of human studies and in the queen of the sciences, physics, have placed new demands upon us to develop a competent logic of inquiry appropriate to our field.

The recognition and formulation of the inadequacy of two-valued logic is described by Leonard Hawes:

> . . . Communication is both the **topic** of research as well as the resource for conducting the research. The implications are fascinating. Communication research is simultaneously referential and reflexive; our work refers to entities outside of the work itself, and at the same time the work is the embodiment of much of what is being studied.[21]

The key terms are "as-well-as" and "simultaneously." This formulation not only is a positive description of communication research practices, but this recognition demands a communicatively competent research criteria which delineates the condition for Hawes' formulation.

20. D. Ehninger, Colloquium at the Ohio State University, February 9, 1978.

21. L.C. Hawes, "The Reflexivity of Communication Research," WESTERN JOURNAL OF SPEECH COMMUNICATION, 1978, 42, pp. 15-16.

The significance of the preceding developments has consequence for the science of communication. A logic of methodology is demanded in which objectivity and the researcher are inextricable. This posits society as a totality and the scientist reflects within this totality. The whole is therefore presupposed before the analytic parts are known. **What are the consequences for communication theory?**

Within the **framework of strict empirical science,** theory designates the interdependent functions of relationships which are formally interpreted as variables of social behavior. "System" and "structural" theories in general attempt to cover the whole social fabric. In the socio-scientific models the deduced relationships between the co-variable quanta are seen as elements of an interdependent system. Yet these constructed systems are not identical with the developing whole and its unfolding process. The concept of system is totally external to the analyzed as are the theoretical statements used to explicate the area. In addition, the introduction of hypothetical statements guarantee the regularity of the area investigated. Therefore, theory must be "isomorphic" to the area of application. On the basis of isomorphism, correspondence between theoretical statements and ontological reality is not known. Theories are at best a schemata of ordering which can be constructed at will and appear as valid for some area when the theory successfully organizes the area.

Since theoretical constructions are not connected in any necessary way with the ontological region, then the connection needs a connector. The connection, according to Jurgen Habermas, is one of **interest** (to someone). Therefore, the indifference of an objective system turns out **not** to be **indifferent** and its application does not give us an empirical objectivity. This objectivity is determined from the viewpoint of epistemological **interest.**[22]

For scientific researchers to become aware that they do not deal with unqualified data introduces the process of **mediation.** The scientific apparatus is social and therefore we must already understand the objects we are about to investigate in order for the categories to remain internal to the object investigated. (This is meaning of an interpretive or communication community.) **Therefore a logic is needed which incorporates the recognition of the sociality of science as well as scientists' self-reflexive awareness of this situation.** This logic we may call three-valued which is formulated by

22. J. Habermas, KNOWLEDGE AND HUMAN INTERESTS (Beacon Press, 1971).

"as-well-as" or "both-and" (being-as-well-as-non-being or both-being-and-non-being). To gain access to this logic I will employ the language of hermeneutics and phenomenology.

The Hermeneutical Imperative

If the human person is social and historical, is it possible to propose a social theory which is not one of the socio-historical events? The appearance of hermeneutics proposes the human is mediated by tradition and the idea of a detached science is in question. The researcher would be living in the socio-historical process immersed in the environment without any possibility of explicating the environment. The hermeneutical notion of society as historical would have to see itself quite paradoxically as ahistorical. **This means that it would no longer be an historical understanding but a trans-cendental condition for all understanding.** The paradox can be represented by the following equation:

$$\frac{\text{hermeneutical}}{\text{transcendental}} = \frac{\text{socio-historical}}{\text{asocial, ahistorical}} = \frac{\text{temporal}}{\text{atemporal}}$$

This means that for socio-historical understanding to become a condition for self-understanding, it must be mediated by its precondition for its awareness; the precondition is the transcendental.

We find ourselves in a precarious situation; while seeking hermeneutical, historical explication of society, we assume an ahistorical (transcendental) vantage point. In turn, were we to explicate the conditions of the meaningful propositions concerning the social life, we would find ourselves in a position of extra-sociality in the transcendental attitude. Paradoxically, we would be engaged in using means for our exposition which are socio-historical. Regardless of the attempts to constitute theoretical and even meta-theoretical structures of social explication, there is an involvement in a wider socio-historical region inexhaustible by the theoretical stance. The understanding of society is not completely obtainable through a socio-theoretical logic nor is it possible to conceive of it purely in hermeneutical-historical terms. Therefore, to ascertain meaningful propositions concerning social communication, an understanding of the transcendental as well as its incorporation into scientific communication research is necessary. The scientific-theoretical process in my opinion is a transcendental approach which essentially accepts the name of meta-theory to carry out its project.

What is the Transcendental Position?

The immediacy of experience and the mediation of this experience stand in a relationship of complementarity. In immediate experience I am not aware that I experience but I deal comprehensively with things and their relationships. If I reflect about my dealings, I **distance** myself from the immediacy of things but with the possibility of the experience of things. **Every theory of epistemology must include a distancing and account for it if it is going to be an inclusive theory.**

Experience is anonymous. The transcendental position brings to relief the conditions; the process of meaning which enables experience to take place. Our thinking and knowledge in its "natural" orientation is at home with the things we attempt to investigate and understand. The transcendental demands a **distancing** from the natural immediacy and in this turn we encounter the problem of how we reflect upon this immediacy. This is the problem we have called mediation. Transcendental understanding simply attempts to discover the meaning of experience. Therefore, as soon as we ask a question concerning the conditions of meaning we are in the transcendental region.

An articulation of how the transcendental functions within the scientific community will aid us in developing a vocabulary for scientific communication theory.

An Explication of the Transcendental: The ahistorical and atemporal

Phenomenology develops out of a critique of psychologism and is a part of the heritage of transcendental philosophy. Transcendental philosophy is a reflection on the possibility of objective knowledge and experience in an attempt to base all sciences on the insights of the governing principles which rule each possible science. Specifically, in the terms of Husserlian phenomenology, the **transcendental functions in the determination of meaning** (or sense-making, as it popularly conceived). The transcendental articulation is mediated (handed down) through a community of linguisticality for each possible science. We find that the transcendental region is mediated by the "sense" or meaning of the speaker, the things in question and an historical residue. This is not convention. Conventions are **already** based on understanding. Therefore a relativist position runs counter to the facts of research and to the communication of such facts to members of the scientific community and the public in general.

The **transcendental functions in the estabalished maxim of cultural and cross cultural studies:** all methods of cultural investigations are based on comparison which includes such phrases as "it is different from . . ." or "it can be understood as . . . ." Comparison involves sameness and difference. This means that the determination of differences by which a culture is distinguished from other cultures assumes a common aspect on the basis of which the differences are seen as differences. Were this not the case, what one would have are differences without any possibility to recognize them as differences from . . . . To recognize differences it is necessary either to assume one of the cultures as a base and interpret others in terms of it or to assume common features across various cultures on the basis of which the variations are comprehensible. The first case cannot be used in cross–cultural studies, since everything would be reduced to the interpretation of the components of one culture missing the structure of other cultures. The only solution to this problem is to show that while cultures are different, they also have commonalities or a possible common dimension from which they may be understood as different. This means that absoluteness and relativity must be correlative.

The **transcendental functions in the identification of data.**[23] For example, only on the basis of the transcendental position can a datum be a possible explanation of laws made through repeated experimentation and subsumed under categories. The transcendental provides the limit for laws and the basis for inductive corrections or falsifications. A datum which moves in a irreversible historical flow, as in the case of field observation studies, is mediated through reflection. Here reflection is not reflection on the "previous" sense data, but on the "reiterated" data, which in the language of phenomenology are eidetic. (We can repeat the data of yesterday only with an identification of the data in terms of a comparative.) **Comparing two data on the basis of a datum which is not on the same level as the ones being compared demands a community of communication with a linguistic habit.** If this logic of identity is social can we have an empirical **social** science as an objective science? Positivism by subsuming this question under the logic of science cannot be a language in either region. Both mediate each other and in turn are mediated. **Therefore, the possibility of social science objectivity is only secured through the understanding of a transcendental logic.** (It is impossible to transcend socio–historical events, but

23. A.B. Fisher, "Evidence Varies with Phrases of Inquiry," WESTERN JOURNAL OF SPEECH COMMUNICATION, 1977, 41, pp. 9-20; J.G. Delia and L. Grossberg, "Interpretation and Evidence, WESTERN JOURNAL OF SPEECH COMMUNICATION, 1977, 41, pp. 32-43.

signification at the transcendental level is **not** correlative to events, point for point.)

The pragmatic-behavioral model of social science, which is the dominant model in the field of communication, presupposes that meaning is identical (point for point) with behavior or the sign = signified.[24] If a behavior is identical to its meaning then for the pragmatic-behavioral model to be inclusive it would be necessary to (a) reduce the observed social habits to a statistical average where truth would be the way that the majority behaves (at least for the time being); and (b) the investigators' procedures would have to be reduced to a habitual pattern and the investigator would have to demonstrate whether he/she fits the pattern of the majority. When signification is identical with behavior, as in the pragmatic-behavioral model of competence, the consequences are:

1. an impossibility to grasp any significance of behavior;

2. the behavior would be closed upon itself;

3. socio-history is incomprehensible;

4. theory would be a behavior which is closed upon itself.

The transcendental function in scientific presentation. Without the transcendental, theory would correspond to the behavior of the writer and to the "predictable social behavior" of one's times. The significance of socio-historical events cannot be explicated in terms of the behavior of such events since it cannot be reduced to, or become identical with, the historical anthropos nor his/her historical praxis. This means that the hermeneutical dimension is a mediation. It delimits the significations appearing historically and socially. Since the significance is the dimension of socio-historical processes constituting the condition for sense-making the understanding of historical events then the hermeneutical process mediates the transcendental region. Hence, the transcendental is a condition for theory and praxis. Therefore, the transcendental is an ahistorical and atemporal. (**Privativum** means to attain a liberation from the temporal or historical.)

Complementarity of Hermeneutics and the Transcendental

The transcendental signification would be impossible without the hermeneutical aspect and would be reduced to the notion of conditions or categories without change or influence. There

---

24. J.W. Bowers, N.D. Elliott, and R.J. Desmond, "Exploiting Pragmatic Rules: Devious Messages," HUMAN COMMUNICATION RESEARCH, 1977, 3, pp. 235-242.

would be a failure to appreciate the articulation of the human event which, in the process of temporal self-interpretation, is also:

1. interpretation of significance (at the transcendental level);

2. constitution of the socio-historical;

3. constitution of reflexivity as a ground for the emergence of inter-subjective relationships.[25]

4. the institution of a social region called theoretical.

We must keep in mind that self-interpretation of the human event is not identical with the behavior of a specific human being. The specific human being understands oneself within the historically mediated transcendental significance constituting the temporality and the atemporality both of permanence and flux of the individual. **This means that reflection and social reflexivity is grounded in the complementarity of hermeneutics and transcendental signification.**

We must not fall into a naive historicism regarding the socio-historical process. Only when we gain **distance** are we able to see our presuppositions which carry an historical aspect of the tradition. To see our presuppositions as historical means that we do not live in the same presuppositions we formally did. To gain such a **distance** and to be able to relate to our former presuppositions assumes a transcendental posture.

Social science research based on communicative competence takes account of its own historical-processes and relates it to the transcendental region of signification which in turn displays: (1) a "vertical distance" from the historicity of events; and (2) the reflexivity for the recognition of historical events.[26] The term "vertical" is employed to convey that the atemporal is perpendicular and sweeps the horizontal stream of the community events.

When the transcendental signification is disregarded, the hermeneutical process assumes an a priori stance without being aware of itself. It assumes a particular historical period and its given events and treats it as if it were the transcendental signification of all historical periods. We must be clear that the transcendental and the hermeneutical aspects are given together. Theoretical reflections reveal one possible

25. J.J. Pilotta, "Presentational Thinking: A Contemporary Hermeneutic of Communicative Action," WESTERN JOURNAL OF SPEECH COMMUNICATION, 1979, 43, pp. 288-300.

26. H.G. Gadamer, TRUTH AND METHOD (Seabury Press, 1975).

hermeneutic of the transcendental signification and specifies at the same time a distance to the socio-historical processes and events. Any theory, seen in terms of its transcendental signification, is absolute. Seen in terms of its hermeneutics, it is relative to other theories. Therefore, the complementarity of the transcendental and the hermeneutical are both **absolute-as-well-as-relative.** Relative is a correlative to something which is absolute and absolute makes sense only in correlation to the relative.

We cannot take the mediating relationship between transcendendental signification and hermeneutics as a relationship between two things. The transcendental is always something that **has been** or is **to be** accomplished through the hermeneutical means. What is accomplished is always reflected from the implications of the future or from the past, therefore the mediation occurs outside real relationships. If this were not the case, theoretical thought would be impossible since all theoretical relationships would be immersed in affectivity nor would we gain the necessary distance to theoretically make sense of socio-historical events.

Hermeneutical criteria are based on the human condition. Whenever we ask a question regarding the sense of social events, powers affecting our lives, or the interpersonal relations among groups, the question points to the transcendental significance. This is a reflection on the question, "what is happening?" which is the genesis of the theoretical.

The search for meaning at the transcendental level, for the purposes of making sense of our socio-cultural environment, constitutes a tension between the interpretation of the factual and the significant. Humans dwell in this tension. Concretely, a person is **simultaneously involved yet distanced from the factual.** This is a movement toward the sense region revealing a particular meaning:

> 1. is not experienced in its totality;
>
> 2. has a situational character;
>
> 3. is oriented which establishes the here-to-there relationship (communicability).

The structure of communicability that we presume suggests that if signification was purely "interpretation," or based purely on the school of pragmatic communication, then interpersonal communication would be impossible. Each person situated in an empirical "here and now" would always be in a different situation and would have to assume the task of repeating the behavior of the other in order to grasp the meaning of the behavior. In fact, the situation of the other has already shifted in its spatio-temporal structure.

Summation

Communicative competence is the condition for social science research. It is the condition which enables reflective distance and the ability to monitor the relationship between the researcher and his/her objects (co-subjects) of investigations. Every investigation presumes a complementarity between the researcher and the researched which is mediated by their respective traditions and their movement toward the extrication of their socio-historical melieu. The movement of extrication toward the transcendental region from meaning is invariant and mediated by the socio-historical. The relationship between the transcendental and hermeneutics reveals a three-valued logic which expands the theory of "scientia." The expanded theory of science is based on acceptability and appropriateness which introduces to the communication-community a social science which is oriented to the determination of the meaningful relationships of social life. Therefore, the structure of the social science community is based on mutual social interaction which demands of itself to be a science of thematic determination (reflexive) and responsibility (socio-historical).

The Dialogical Region

Algis Mickunas

There is a great deal of effort, emotion, formalism and ink spilt across the pages analyzing the meaning of linguistic terms and propositions. Yet, there is very little said about the functioning of such terms and propositions in the communicative-dialogical process and the implications for experience and the constitution of interpersonal understanding. Phenomenology and hermeneutics, in their turn, assume the question of communication in terms of inter-subjectivity, the experience of the other, and in terms of history which consists of a pregiven "text" in whose "fluidum" the human lives.

In the phenomenological tradition a number of scholars have investigated the process of communication in terms of dialogue: S. Strasser, H.H. Schrey, C.A. van Peursen, B. Waldenfels, and E. Minkowski. In all of these works concerning the dialogical process there is an "implicit" separation between dialectics and dialogue. Dialectics is based on an initial judgement, **Ur-teil**, an "initial separation and unification of subject and predicate,"[1] while dialogical thought is founded in a field of interactions of subject-subject and world where separation and unification constitute only one kind of relationship; the judgemental relationship. My discussion will focus on the topics of the (a) triadic relationship of the dialogical region, (b) the policentric structure of the perceptual field, (c) the role of body in communication, and (d) the temporal-historical dimension of dialogue. While the topics are differentiated analytically, in the actual

INTERPERSONAL COMMUNICATION: Essays in Phenomenology and Hermeneutics, ed., Joseph J. Pilotta, Copyright 1982, The Center for Advanced Research in Phenomenology, Inc. and co-published by arrangement with The University Press of America, Inc.

1. Ludwig Landgrebe, PHANOMENOLOGIE UND GESCHICHTE (Wissenschaftliche Buchgesellschaft, 1968), p. 95.

dialogical process they are inextricable. (Our treatment of the various topics will not be "pure" and will contain elements of the rest of the topics.)

The Triadic Structure of Dialogue

Schrey suggests that certain conditions must be met if human dialogue is to make sense at all, theoretically. First, it is essential to avoid the reduction of all experience to an "ego-centric" subject, in the sense that a subject becomes the ultimate arbiter of others and the world. Second, it is necessary to abandon the modern concept of "collectivity" in which the individual is merely a function in the midst of intersecting social forces.[2] To avoid reductionism to an ego-centric subjectivism, where the ego establishes the meaning of the world and the dialogical partner, the following principles are to be maintained:

1. The upper limit of dialogue is transgressed if a common core of meaning of events or things becomes a sole possession of one of the dialogical partners with a capacity to constitute meaning inaccessible to others.

2. The lower limit of dialogue is transgressed if the dialogical partners are interpreted in terms of senders and receivers of sound waves, visual stimuli or conditioned by the environment. In such mechanistic interpretations, the dialogical partners cannot occupy the same spatial position at the same time and hence do not have precisely the same stimuli and environment. What one experiences is in principle inaccessible to the other and what one communicates is either incomprehensible to the other or is understood by the other in terms of one's own stimuli and environment. In the latter case one does not understand what the other says, but only what the environment dictates; therefore, communication fails.

3. Even if an assumption is made that the dialogical partners possess a common world of things and events, the dialogical process is disrupted if the world is signified differently by the individual communicators. Only the engagement in a common signification, in a common meaning, which remains constant across the variations of subjective and objective states, guarantees the continuity of the dialogical process.

The crucial aspect of the dialogical theory of communication is "signification"; the meaning-giving activity of the dialogical partners. "Signification" in this context is a process which "means" something **other than itself,** a direction toward

2. H.H. Schrey, DIALOGISCHES DENKEN (Wissenschaftliche Buchgesellschaft, 1970), p. IX.

something or other which is meant. The process is such that the meaning is not identical with the meant. Yet, the meaning and the meant object or event are always related to one another. For example, an act of perception of a table "means" the table, is an oriented act, yet the act of meaning and the meant table are distinct. The table can be meant as an antique, as a spatial object to be measured or as an object serving practical purposes. The disassociation and correlation between the meaning and the meant is usually more complex. It is possible to mean objects of distinct genera in one or various ways. For example, a table, a book, a person and a painting can be meant as a "group of objects," a "set of distinct entities," or "examples of social institutions." The various things may be replaced, and yet such things may be signified in terms of the same meanings. What is communicated or remains constant through the variations of things and events, is their **meaning**. We must recall that meaning always designates the meant. In this sense things and events constitute exchangeable examples of meanings without dictating a particular meaning they exemplify. **The communicative process is an aim at a common meaning which is without spatio-temporal or environmental restrictions and need not change with variations in the spatio-temporal phenomena, and thus is capable of maintaining the constancy required for communication.** While we cannot go back to yesterday's events, we can communicate the way those events were meant.

While the above requirements of the dialogical process are to be respected, the dialogical domain has a precise structure. It consists of (1) the significative orientation to a state of affairs, things or events by the dialogical partners; (2) an orientation of the dialogical partners to each others in terms of the signification or meaning of the things or events (and not to the other as an entity in a field of orientations); (3) an orientation of the dialogical partners to themselves. I orient myself to someone for the sake of something, work with the other on something, speak to the other about something, therefore establishing a position with respect to something and to the other. This "eidetic" structure remains constant through various interpretations and must be maintained if the dialogical domain is to continue. Even when I communicate with the other about myself or about him/her, one of us becomes an object of our mutual orientation and signification. The novelty of the dialogical relationship consists in its disruption of the binary relationship between self and world or between self and other as an object in a field of objects.

The other attains a particular position in dialogue; speaking spatially, the other has a locus **not** facing someone and **not** being a background experiential process like a self, but is "next to the other." The other (originally present) is not an object toward which one is oriented, but co-functions in all orientations and significations. It is not the other who is thematic but what the other says, signifying the meant events and things, what the other speaks about, acts upon, and perceives. As Husserl indicates, "It is not the other that is thematic but what the other says when I am in a position to understand and incorporate what he says. The co-presence of the other is for me a co-presence and we are at something in a unity of function."[3]

The act of turning toward the other is not similar to acts dealing with objects. The object motivates the other in terms of what the object is as signified (meant). One does something with it without its taking any initiative to the actor or the experiencing speaker. The relationship to an object is not a co-operation, co-orientation or mutual signification; if an object were to become such, it would be a fetish. The other is not an object but an addressee of one's comportment, a receiver or a sender of the meaning of something. The mode of turning to the other is one of addressing, contesting or evoking. As Waldenfels says, "Here the vocative sense comes to the fore."[4] The encounter of the other in a dialogue is not a confrontation of two subjectivities attempting to read external signs produced by each in order to decipher what lurks in the other's "interiority," but is a primordial **presence** prior to any distinction between interior and exterior states. It is a presence "read" in terms of a third aspect; the things and events signified in the dialogical process. This is exemplified by an interrogative dialogue.

If we keep in mind the triadic dialogical structure, it is possible to show how in the dialogical process speaking and counter speaking dissolve and incorporate one another. While the initiative may shift from one speaker to the other, lending one or the other an active role, there is no sharp demarcation between activity and passivity. Speaking and counter-speaking is one event with various phases. Question and answer are unified in a double movement initiated by the questioner and reaching its aim in the counter movement of receiving an answer. A counter movement coming from the listener fulfills itself in a communication of an answer. Thus the movement and counter movement are delimited from the outset by the dialogical aim. When one addresses the other about something, one assumes initiative and becomes "active." But what does it mean to say "active?" While addressing

---

3. Edmund Husserl, MANUSCRIPT A V 5, 1932, p. 109.

4. Behnard Waldenfels, DAS ZWISCHENREICH DES DIALOGS: Sozial Philosophische Untersuchungen in Anschlissan E. Husserl (Martinus Nijhoff, 1971), p. 139.

someone, while asking a question actively, one is already passively expecting an answer which fulfills the question and at the same time contains an **aura** of possibilities: acceptance, rejection, correction or perhaps a rephrasing of the question. This complex is contained in the dialogical domain from its inception. Activity and passivity are completely intertwined. Every initiation is already an expectation, and every expectation contains a possibility for reinitiation. By initiating the dialogue, the speaker at the same time lends to the listener a co-initiative to listen and reply and for the speaker to become a co-listener.

The same dialogical requirements are present in listening. The passivity of listening is not a precursory step for a subsequent activity of responding but is an initiation. In receptivity the listener already knows that he/she is propelled toward an answer, toward a presence of a field containing possibilities wherein one's answer is accepted, rejected, understood or questioned. One's passivity is already an active engagement in the dialogical field which is **open** and **delimited** by possibilities of signification and re-signification.

The dialogical process does not create a commonality of the signification of events and things but unfolds it. A mutual engagement in dialogue assumes a domain of common meaning which can be illuminated or obscured. It is a condition for the possibility of dialogue requiring an "identical sense," a unitary attentional core,[5] with a continuously identifiable meaning given through various alterations of addressing, listening, formulating, rejecting, accepting and understanding. This unitary core of meaning lends stability and continuity to the dialogical process. Simultaneously, the signified things and events comprise the perceptual exemplification of what is being meant factually. In this sense all significations have an orientation toward the factual (perceptual entities). The dialogical partners assume what each other means and realizes the meaning either in direct perception, imagination or in memory. The factual and significative aspects intersect at this juncture. The factual, while being signified by the dialogical partners in various ways, is suggestive of other possible significations. The **empirical** domain is never out of the question; rather it is the very content and extension of meaning. The presence of the factual content is essential for the temporal and spatial extension of the dialogical region. Subsequently, the factual dimension is the very embodiment of meaning.

5. Edmund Husserl, IDEEN I (Martinus Nijhoff, 1950), p. 230.

Time and Unity of the Dialogical Domain

Husserl observes that the unity of the dialogical partners is given in everyday experience. "In mutual understanding my experiences and acquisitions encounter those of the other as my own series of experience within my experiential life."[6] Yet such a unity requires the role of time. Question and answer, speaking and response, appears not only in relationship to the signified objectivity, but also within a temporal interrelationship occurring passively in a common process. The present speaking is but a phase of a dialogue. In speaking at the present the partners maintain a co-presence of the phases which occurred and which are about to occur: while passively listening and formulating an answer to a question, the just asked question continues to be co-present with the present formulation and with the actual voicing of an answer. And the initial question and answer may retain their presence throughout the dialogue. The coming phases also have a co-presence in the current phases. This process expands into a common temporal field with its inde-terminate–determinable horizons. The horizons of the dialogical process are not always covered point for point by the partners. The open possibilities for signification may vary from partner to partner leading to a partial covering and leaving the field for a continuous synthesis and variation. This process is also exposed to possible fragmentation. If temporal possibili-ties are introduced which resignify the dialogue in a different manner, the process is disrupted and a new theme is taken up leading to new syntheses. The term "synthesis" means that in the changes of opinions, articulations, and modes of percep-tions, there emerges an identical core of meaning which makes sense of the variations. Such a core accounts for the partial covering of the temporal horizons of significations of the dialogical partners. Their activities constitute a "unified relationship,"[7] a policentrically articulated total movement of transitional experiences, changing intentionalities, com-prising "a context of expanded and encompassing common con-sciousness."[8] In the temporal structuration of the policen-tric field there emerges a unity of a "supra–personal con-sciousness."[9]

The "supra–personal consciousness" and the "poli-centric field" have a specific shape. In order to maintain the individuality and synthesis of meaning of the dialogical partners in

6. Ibid., KRISIS, p. 166.

7. Edmund Husserl, IDEEN II (Martinus Nijhoff, 1952), p. 192.

8. Ibid., KRISIS, p. 166.

9. Edmund Husserl, GEMEINGEIST II, p. 17.

principle it is impossible to begin with an organismic social consciousness wherein the individual is absorbed. The individual would not count as a contributor to the dialogical process. It is also impossible to begin with a radical egology where relationships are external without any guarantees of commonality. Only in the dialogical domain do we encounter a locus of a constitution of commonality founded on immanent relationships of meaning of independent personalities. This communality is actualized in communication where the partners confront the same core of meaning of events and objects. This signification is a "higher unity," a **founded whole.** A founded whole consists of parts which are given only in relation to the others. A distinction must be made between a pervasive unity in which dependent parts are founded one in the other (tone quality and intensity), and where independent parts found a new content, e.g., the ones build a new melody.[10] The latter unity is similar to the dialogical domain constituting a "supra-consciousness." It is a complex formation of significations having a continuous relationship to the dialogical partners. The significations of the one are mediated and thus appropriated by the acts of the other. Like the notes, the acts found the unitary meaning, although the latter is not identical to the acts. This founding can be assumed by various other means: arts, rituals, codes of interaction and diverse institutions. The individual, without a loss of individuality, becomes a carrier and transmitter of a tradition.

The field of significations, comprising variations in the constitution of a unitary meaning, allows each dialogical partner to assume an encompassing role. Each partner "borrows" the experience of the other and expands his/her own experience through the other. This implies that one's experiences and sensibilities are extended by the presence and interactions of the experiences and sensibilities of the others. Experiences are extended not merely by those who are actually present, but of those whose experiences had intertwined with ours in the past and were transmitted through various institutionalized carriers. Each individual has his/her own sensibilities, apperceptions and enduring unities, while the communicating community, the "poli-centered field,"[11] in its own right has sensibilities, significations and a continuous mode of perception with a correlative world of indeterminate horizons. I see and hear not only with my senses but also with those of the others and they with mine. This is a way that consciousness is in its activities and passivities in relationship to others. In this sense each individual in the field of

10. Edmund Husserl, LOGISCHE UNTERSUCHUNGEN (Halle, 1913), pp. 21-22.

11. Ibid., GEMEINGEIST II, p. 18.

dialogue can orient himself/herself not only toward his/her own experiences, but also toward "our" experiences and consciousness. Thus each individual comprises one center, one point of orientation, one set of experiences which are propagated through the experiences of others, and those of others through his/hers: the dialogical domain is thus a poli-centric domain of "we-consciousness" founded in "I-consciousness." Yet the "I-consciousness" is expanded through the "we-consciousness."

The founded dialogical process serves for all as an index of manifold significations and possible perceptions of objects and events. What is experienced in communication by the one at the present is seen as having been experienced or just about to be experienced by the other and conversely. In this transition, one experiences his/her own perceptions as the realizations of the significations of the other and the perceptions of the other as realization of one's own significations. Therefore, prior to any expressed understanding there is already a pregiven unification of experiences in the dialogical process. What is present to others is also present to me in the process of distinguishing my own perspective from those of the others. I borrow the vision, the perception of the others to see the same thing signified some other way, "from there" and "from then." Such sensibilities extend to include the entire institutional and historical framework. In this sense, the entire traditions may constitute the "supra-individual consciousness" which is nonetheless maintained through the individual partners who carry and orient such traditions as a poli-centric dialogical domain.

Concrete Expression

The outlined configuration of the dialogical domain requires mediation through a concrete linguistic tradition and human gesture. A linguistic tradition specifies the dialogical field of significations and limits it to a set of concrete expressions. These traditionally habituated expressions and linguistic procedures have their own modes of passivity, activity, pliability and rigidity, stressing some meanings, rejecting others, while unifying and dispersing perceptual processes with their semantic and syntactic requirements. The dialogical process of signification has a universality, which submits to the conditions of a situation: the historically developed linguistic capacities, the expressive abilities of the dialogical partners and the immediate concerns of the cultural-natural environment.

In the final analysis, corporeal expression and gesture constitute a commitment to a situation, an anchorage in a milieu, an immersion in an environment and an attunement of a field of action. Corporeity is a "being toward the world constituting a pre-objective and pre-subjective experience."[12] It is primarily an active dimension and the world is experienced in terms of orientations of activities (human and otherwise). Signification assumes a corporeal and situational rooting and the very structure of corporeal action is intertwined.

While situatedness and orientation is a principle of limitation, corporeity, due to its power of signification, is also a principle of transcendence: (a) transcendence towards the universality of meaning: woman already means mother, wife, mistress, sweetheart, tsarina, and madona; and (b) spatio-temporal transcendence. While signifying a particular event by corporeal gesture, the event assumes various spatio-temporal directions. Various vectors interconnect with other events of the past and those to come. Universality of meaning and factual uniqueness, localization and orientational directions intersect and are revealed in the corporeal schema. In addition to being a limitation, corporeity is also an initiation, a signification, a "transcendence in **status nascendi**."[13] The conjunction of limitation and transcendence, universality and fact occurs in corporeal signification. Landgrebe has shown corporeity makes factual events and meaning, concrete objects and essential structures mutually implicative, in a manner which allows concrete events and objects an essentiality of their own.[14]

While corporeal concrete gestures play an important role in the communication of the events and objects in the experiential field, the field itself has its own communicative process. Events and objects are not locked within their present spatio-temporal moment. They relate to each other, point to and have orientations among one another. They comprise a field of vectors, forces and tensions having their proper meaning. A sapling reveals the force of the storm, its own resiliency and the calmness of the day. The deer, carefully sniffing the air, reveals or points to the presence of danger or a watering place. Our gestures do not project a meaning on the field, but trace it, elicit it from latency, a latency possessing **more** meaning than any specific gesture could exhaust. Is the deer sniffing for danger or water, for foliage or mate? Our communication about one of these possible meanings does not exhaust the field. That is why each gesture in a field, each spoken word and its meaning are not complete, but is always tensed toward **more** which is present

12. M. Merleau-Ponty, PHENOMENOLOGIE DE LA PERCEPTION (Gallimard, 1969).

13. W. Mueller, ETRE-AU-MONDE (Bouvier Verlag, 1975), p. 125.

14. See note 1, p. 46ff.

in the field. The field constantly demands more of our gestures, and in the dialogical process the partners aid each
other in eliciting the more; explicating what is latent in
the interconnected field. The dialogical process is complemented
by and intertwined with the communicative process of the
field in which the dialogical partners are engaged.

The communicative power of corporeity is co-equal with the
communicative process of the field. The bodily gesture tracing
a shooting star across the sky means the shooting star, while
the shooting star with its orientation elicits the meaning of
the gesture. Merleau-Ponty has shown that the field is not
something confronted by the gesture; rather it is immanent
in every gesture and signification. For instance, in a game
the body constitutes a unity with the total movement of the
game wherein each aspect of the game communicates other
aspects. Each play pattern communicates certain requirements
of the corporeal gesture, and with each shift of corporeal
movements the entire field is reconstructed into new spatio-
temporal vectors. Each gesture not only signifies the field,
but is also signified by it by its own shifting requirements.
The vectors, the movements and the lines of force within the
field are **latent** with expectations which transcend the
immediacy of the game and yet which play a role in the
current movement of our corporeal gestures. The lines of communication of the game as a field of action are directly intertwined with corporeal signification.

In terms of the dialogical process, the dialogical partners
are engaged in signifying a common field which, while
eliciting their gestures, has more latent meaning than the
dialogue could exhaust. At the same time the partners are
completely de-centered from their own ego-centric stances and
are intertwined in the field and its communicative process.
This is not to say that they are completely subsumed in the
field; rather, with their shifts of significations and perceptions, as parts of the field, the field as such is affected,
is manifested in its different meanings and horizonal implications. The corporeal communicative power is two sided: while
moving with its own gestures to signify the field, the field
calls forth the gestures appropriate to a given situation.
Corporeity with its expressive gestures signifies both, the
field in communication and its own posture toward the field.
But the posture cannot be read without the field. Corporeity
is the rooting of the signifying self and at the same time
an articulation of the communicative movements and vectors
of the field. In this sense, the human dialogue is also a
field dialogue.

The concrete, corporeal encounter in the dialogical process is a constant upsurgence toward the experiential field. The dialogical partner is decipherable directly in terms of the gestures elicited by the vectors, the plains of actions, the forces of the field yielding the significance of the gestures and the other's unique mode of signifying something. The gesture is effaced before the signified aspects of the field and the position of the gesture makes sense only in relationship to such aspects. The dialogical partners are primarily engaged in a field of action, at a task or a discussion of something. The perspectives blend and cross at the horizon, at the task, where significations converge to form a unitary process constantly exposed to disruption by the factors in the field establishing new orientations and calling for re-signification.

The corporeal gesture and expression possess a sedimented style. The style is propagated by the corporeity of the other in dialogue. Such fleeting expressions as sadness, wonder, rejection by a look of disbelief, etc. all are directly assumed by the other and continued either by showing of concern, interrogation or simply immersion in the same expressive style. Even if a different style is taken up by the other, it is possible to read the style in a unitary process of a dialogue. The lighting up of a face with joy may be directly taken up by another in a question, or continued in the same joy. Corporeal expressivity is dialogically inter-corporeal.

Dialogue and History

As already noted, the dialogical domain is dominated by temporal process. Space, as the other basic dimension of the concrete world, is structured primarily by temporal experience. Nearness and distance are primarily temporal possessions of the world. The distant in space is the possible in the nearing future. Somewhere else is where one has been or somewhere is where one may be. This sort of temporality is also the ground of the corporeal capacity to transcend to the "other side" of objects. While speaking about the other side, one traces temporal and spatial vectors about something which is to be seen from "then and there." Hence the field of action with its vectors, forces and movement orientations is both temporal and spatial. This temporal dimension allows for the "borrowing" of perceptions from dialogical partners, both present and absent, resulting in a poli-centric field which is not bound by the present situation but can extend historically. The dialogical partners can raise such questions as: "How did Cicero view the situation?" or "viewed in terms of Aristotelian categories this aggregate of parts could be seen as a substance." Transmitted through institutionalized means, Cicero's and Aristotle's perceptions can become parts of the dialogue and extend the perceptions of the dialogical partners. although seemingly abstract, such "borrowing" of institutionalized transmission of views, changes the concrete perceptions of the dialogical partners. This means that historically institutionalized expressions, transmitted through such means as language, ritual, social organization, modes of education, etc., are parts of the field of action. They are habitual ways in which we signify and trace the solicitations of the field.

The temporal ability to borrow perceptions from times past is the ground of history as a dialogical dimension. But history adds two aspects to the dialogical process: (a) the individual is never removed from a dialogical situation. By being born in a particular linguistic milieu, the individual is always in a poly-centric field transmitted through language. (b) the historically transmitted modes of dialogue, modes of signification and perception are highly selective; they include a limited range of possible significations and perceptions. This is not to say that the limits cannot be broken; rather, the limits are transgressed. The historical process of culturation is an anonymous structuration of our perceptions and modes of signification. Yet the anonymous power is not an abstract notion such as "society" or "spirit of the times." It appears in the corporeal gestures and is inter-corporeal. Since corporeity is the locus of signification and manifestation of the field of action, and since the historical dimension enters with its sedimented modalities of signification and perception, then the concrete corporeal expressions in the dialogical process are imbued both with the interconnected requirements of the field and with the historically transmitted modes of signifying, selecting and perceiving the interconnections. Hence, the natural-corporeal gestures and expressions and the natural acts of perception are constantly imbued with the historical-cultural **depth** of significations and perceptions.

The historically transmitted cultural modalities of speaking are assumed by the members of a community; thus at the very outset the members are dialogical in a concrete inter-corporeal manner. Inter-corporeal dialogue is a manifestation of the requirements of the perceptual field and of the historically-cultural transmissions of meaning. This means: the corporeal process in a dialogue is more than can be grasped empirically and intellectually. The significations of corporeity can be inscribed in institutions which in their turn constitute a set of concrete and interconnected web of significations. Concrete institutions, as well as the field of action, comprise a field of historically sedimented expressions. This is not just a sum of bricks, but a school, signifying modes of action and orientation. The institutions are embodiments of meaning with their vectors, lines of force and direction. They are our "historical body" and our dialogical process with one another assumes its presence. One could say that the institutions are significative extensions of our corporeal power to express itself in a field of action. As our own gestures of signification prolong themselves in concrete institutions, as our perceptions and expressions inhabit the rituals, schools, poetic announcements, the institutions in turn prolong themselves in our gestures of dialogical encounter, with one another and with the institutionally transmitted modes of comportment.

The dialogical domain is a conjunction of the cultural-historical and the natural. The conjunction is such that it is impossible to extricate one from the other. While attempting to signify the field and its vectors, the gesture also traces historically institutionalized meaning with various open possibilities. While using historically sedimented meanings and perceptions, the gesture discovers that the meanings and perceptions are partially distorted by the field and its open horizons. The dialogical domain is an intersection of the historical-cultural and the natural. In the natural, we find the shape of the other. For example, when we use a hammer, we find wood, but wood shaped by the other into a handle. The hammer communicates the entire milieu. It implicates not only the other, but a mode of production of implements and their use. Their use is in turn a system of communication among various factors: the hammer points to a nail, the nail to a board, the board to a wall, and the wall to a house to be inhabited by erotically charged newlyweds.

The dialogical domain includes the communicative interconnections of the fields of nature and culture. Besides our own power to express, signify and transcend the limitations of the immediate situation. The two fields have also the capacity of mutual significative interactions, constantly pointing beyond the immediate restrictions toward the **more**; what has been and what is to come. Even sciences attempt to practice this kind of transcendence by "reading the signs" of natural events in terms of the historically transmitted modes of statistical calculations.

Summary

The phenomenological approach to dialogue is an attempt to decipher the experiential structures required for human communication and at the same time to show the concrete filling of the structures within the "natural and cultural" fields of action. Although our discussion did not include such factors as "face to face" human interactions, a kind of direct observation of one dialogical partner by the other, our intent was to present a more fundamental and originary dimension of the dialogical process. Indeed a dialogue can occur between two persons exploring one another in an erotically entranced way, yet such explorations are already founded on the prior immersion in the "natural-cultural fields" toward and in terms of which the dialogical partners are oriented. The triadic process of self-field-self is maintained as prior to any direct interpersonal encounter. Even the interpersonal encounter assumes the triadic structure. I am talking to the other **about** him/her or about myself. There is the intentional orientation toward someone, the other or myself, yielding the essential structure of the dialogue.

The positive aspects of dialogical understanding allow us to give a full due to the field of action, to historically developed culture and at the same time to the individual contributors. The individual is not the sole arbiter of the world and culture and in turn, the world and culture do not abolish the individual. Phenomenologically, the dialogical process avoids both the cultural-natural determinism and the autocracy of the ego. It also provides a way toward the unity and diversity of the dialogical partners which allows for mutual understanding as well as diverse positions and points of view. But, at bottom, the human world and the human are dialogical.

The Experience of Media

Don Ihde

In this essay I shall examine some of the perceptual aspects of interpersonal communication, particularly as they become embodied through technological media. In today's complex and technologically textured world an increasingly important dimension of communications occur precisely through such media. The important question is how the effects of such media change or transform the communication situation, particulary our most basic perceptions of media. In undertaking this inquiry here I shall vary both non-Mediated or face-to-face communications situations with those which are technologically embodied through media proper. The primary conceptual tools I shall use in this examination are those derived from phenomenology and I shall begin by taking account of a range of perceptually variable situations with respect to human communication with our world and each other.

Some years ago certain psychologists conducted what were known as sensory deprivation experiments. The design of the experiment was such that the subject's usual sensory opening to the world was presumably closed off and he was placed in an environment in which he could make no discriminations concerning that environment. Thus his eyes were sealed; ears stopped up; he was placed in a weightless state suspended in warm water at a temperature such that he could not even tell where his bodily limit was in relation to the water. Under these extreme conditions in which there was no distinct "world" to which to relate, the subjects would begin to hallucinate vividly after only a short time. Subjects reported hearing

INTERPERSONAL COMMUNICATION: Essays in Phenomenology and Hermeneutics, ed., Joseph J. Pilotta, Copyright 1982, The Center for Advanced Research in Phenomenology, Inc. and co-published by arrangement with The University Press of America, Inc.

voices and seeing people often arrayed in cartoon-like fashion before them and usually in some cinema-like random succession.

The subjects (or victims) of this experiment could be classed into two extreme groups with respect to the results. At one extreme the subjects were so disturbed that even long after the experiment they were found to be in a state approximating psychosis, while at the other extreme (and mostly for those who knew what to expect) the experience was merely reported as entertaining.

Apart from the questionable ethic of performing such extreme experiments, there are several interesting points which can be used in this context to point up certain analogies with the experience of media. Indeed, I shall use these analogies to introduce the major topic of this essay, a phenomenology of the experience of contemporary media.

The first and shallowest analogy regards the similarity of the hallucinatory display to many contemporary audio-visual media such as cinema. The subjects reported a march of sometimes surrealistic images, often in cartoon form, in a parade of apparently disconnected or at most random "plots." The capacity of audio-visual media to break up the normal sequences of the auditory and visual dimensions of perception and to rearrange these at will is a familiar effect in contemporary television and cinema. Time reversals, flash-backs, jumping from one scene to another, disjunctions and juxtapositions are virtually the normal fare for such media.

Secondly, however, there would seem to be a quite different response between the ordinary viewer of a spectacle and the victim of the sensory deprivation experiment. We would not ordinarily expect television to elicit a quasi-psychotic state in the viewer. But a slight variation upon the history of viewing shows something closer to the analogy than appears at first sight. Today's replays of "horror movies" of the classic sort are responded to by today's jaded viewers as mild amusement. Frankenstein, Dracula and ghouls and zombies today appear naive and ridiculous. But yesterday's viewers apparently found them more genuinely frightening. Thus like the subjects who know what to expect in contrast to those who did not, an approximation of the difference between threatened psychosis and mere entertainment emerges in the history of viewing.

There is yet more which can be instructively drawn from the phenomenon of sensory deprivation experiments for purposes here, particularly through a beginning phenomenological interpretation of the experiment. The phenomenologist claims that all human experience has an essential and invariant shape which he calls **intentionality**. By this he means that experience is directed, focused, shaped in such a way that it refers, points to and culminates in a **world**. A world, minimally, is an environment which surrounds one, but which is also "other" than one. Intentionality, then, is that experiential "space" which simultaneously distances us and involves us with world.

The sensory deprivation experiment radically reduces the usual richness of the world which is filled with everything from cabbages to kings and more, and in terms of a partial phenomenological point, attempts to reduce the subject's experience to a "worldless" state. But, secondly, phenomenology interprets intentionality as not only a distance from and involvement in world, but as **reflexive** with respect to world. This is to say that the shape of our experience is such that, at bottom, what we eventually come to know of ourselves is strictly reciprocal with what we come to know of the world. Without world there would be no self; without self no experience of world. Thus the phenomenologist should not be surprised that the result of the experiment is the emergence of a "hallucinatory world." The basic relation of human to world must be maintained if there is to be any self-identity. Thus if the so-called external, perceptual world recedes, the active constituting phase of intentionality will create its own "world." (Here there may even be a clue for the pathologies of intentionality. A patient who rejects, fears, is anxious over the dimension of the world we might take to be ordinary, can also retreat into the "world" of the hallucinatory.) But the main point is, that so long as there is experience the phenomenologist holds that it will have intentional shape in the form of a complex human world correlation. And inversely, the simultaneous distance-involvement with the world is reflexive in such a way that for every item in the world there is some possible reflexion back toward the self.

To signify in simple form this basic phenomenological principle, I offer the formalism:

$$\text{Human} \longrightarrow \text{World}$$

Here human is the experiencer; the arrow signifies the intentional distance-involvement; the world is the terminus or fulfillment of the experiential aim. The reflexive structure of intentionality, then, can be signified by noting the way in which world is taken back into my self-experience with a second arrow making intentionality interactive:

$$\text{Human} \underset{\longleftarrow - - -}{\xrightarrow{}} \text{World}$$

It should be noted that in its most extreme form, phenomenology makes what is called a "transcendental" claim
concerning this as an invariant structure of human experience, but for our purposes here it is sufficient to merely
note that human denotes any possible human experience related
to the world-correlate interpreted as any possible world-
state.

In yet another allusion to the sensory deprivation experiment,
when that whole range of experience which normally and
familiarly we take to be the "external" world is cut off, the
shape of intentionality is modified such that a different
"world" reoccurs. In short, whereas intentionality remains
constant in this interpretation, the modification of both world
and human correlates change. Moreover the change or modification itself is one in which if there is some modification
at one side, there is an implied change to be located on the
other.

There is one other feature of this preliminary phenomenological
model which needs to be related to the sensory deprivation
experiment. When the subject's normal relations with world
have been cut off, a hallucinatory "world" emerges as if in
compensation. What this phenomenon points to is not only
the apparent need for humans to have a world, but to the
global character of a normal perceptual world. Perception
is normally global, wholistic and is a filled plenum. (Upon
a closer analysis of sensory deprivation one would note that
perception remains constant even under those extreme conditions although by being dimmed down the perceptual correlate clearly becomes disturbing to some. The stopping of ears
and the closing of eyes does not cause perception to cease,
but merely dims down and dampens our distinct traffic with
the environment.) Thus in the experiment the compensation
of hallucinations, ever richer and more multi-dimensioned,
begin to replace the dimmed down perceptions.

Metaphorically one can say that not only is intentionality
constant, but that any gaps or reduced dimensions are
enriched by other means. Here we find a clue to the magic
of early radio. Fans of radio drama could be just as hypno-
tized as today's youth sitting before the television, but what
was lacking in terms of visuals was, more than made up by
the compensation of the vivid imagination which accompanied
radio drama. Thus attempts to visualize Batman were bound
to be failures just as the visualization of good novels fails
since they cannot approximate the active intentionality of
imaginative compensation. This filling of the empty dimensions

of media, however, has always been recognized as **my** activity. The special and private "world" of the listener carries the sense of revery or a partial dream-like state which enhances the entertainment.

The above illustrations point up the minimal set of operative notions from phenomenology which can now be applied to the inquiry into the experience of media. What remains is to isolate and delimit the inquiry so as to detect the salient features of the transformations of experience which media make possible. In so doing I wish to introduce a technical interpretation of what shall count as a medium for purposes of this essay: A medium, as I shall use it here, will include (a) some material artifact which is experientially used in a particular way to (b) convey what may be called broadly an expressive activity. Thus the ordinary sense of media, such as newspapers, radio, cinema, television, will be preserved as in each case there is an artifact or set of artifacts (technologies) which are used to convey information, messages, entertain, stimulate or arouse.

Such media may be said, in normative use, to **embody** expressive activity and to embody it by means of some **materialization** which may include word, image, action, reproduction, representation or whatever. I shall exclude from my notion of media the ordinary though somewhat strange usage of an art form as a medium. Someone who performs a dance is performing and expressing; the dance is the expression and thus I will not consider the dance to be a "medium." Instead, a medium will necessarily be something which is between the expressor of the expressive activity and the recipient just as the spiritualist medium is presumably "between" the living and the dead. By being situated between the direct expressive activity and the recipient a medium inherently occupies a potentially **hermeneutic** role. (The hermeneut is an interpreter, for example the priest or oracle who conveys the messages of the gods.)

By so defining the media-situation—a definition which I think will be seen to be appropriate to the phenomenon—I also may relate media to the phenomenological understanding of intentionality. The non-mediated situation may be symbolized as follows:

$$\text{Human} \rightleftharpoons \text{World}$$

In this symbolization the intentional interaction with the world may be described as **direct**. What I have in mind are what can be called direct perceptual situations which I shall term **face-to-face** situations. Here normal human dialogue may be taken as the paradigm. When you and I speak face to face our mutual experience is directed towards each other. The perceptual situation is such that the full play of the senses is open--I see your gestures; hear your intonations; feel your expressive presence, etc. Such a situation is unmediated. Thus in such situations I shall not speak of media.

If, however, I were to speak to you over a telephone, the situation is dramatically altered. In this case the dialogue is not face-to-face, but mediated by means of the telephone. The telephone as a medium is **between** us. This may be symbolized with respect to intentionality thusly:

$$\text{Human} \underline{\hspace{2cm}} \text{medium} \underline{\hspace{2cm}} \rightarrow \text{World}$$
$$(\ \text{I} \underline{\hspace{2cm}} \text{telephone} \underline{\hspace{2cm}} \rightarrow \text{you}\ )$$

What this formalism takes account of is a medium in **mediating position.** The artifact (telephone) is taken into intentionality and occupies a mediating position. I have elsewhere developed a phenomenology of instrumentation which takes account of certain key features of such mediation, but only a few of these features are needed here to apply to media.[1]

First, note that the medium of the telephone is such that it may be said to embody the dialogue; it makes your voice present to me and mine to you. In so doing the artifact when functioning well "withdraws" as Heidegger says, or becomes semi-transparent. At optimum function, I am able to recognize your voice as yours and although your presence to me is **reduced** perceptually to a mere voice, the presence is one in "real space-time." This capacity of a medium to materialize us to each other in spite of vast geographical distances, is, of course, one of the advantages of media. But at the same time the advantage is gained at a price. Your presence to me through the telephone is--compared to global perception--a reduced presence and lacking in the perceptual richness of the face-to-face situation. Furthermore, if all I need is information, the telephone seems relatively adequate; but if you are my wife or other intimate, while the immediacy of the telephone is better than the more "abstract" letter, there remains a sense of lack. (Here imaginative compensations may occur to fill in the experience, but in contrast to the possibility of genuine face-to-face contact these remain only a partial satisfaction.) Here we begin to sense what might be called a center of gravity to a given medium, a center which is only relatively adequate to some purposes and less so with respect to others.

1. Don Ihde, TECHNICS AND PRAXIS (Reidel Publishers, 1979).

And even if the telephone permits genuine embodiment of a real space-time dialogue, it does not do so without transforming that dialogue. The space-time of a telephone conversation has a certain **irreal** character to it as well. For example, the space-time of such a conversation is always that of a **near distance.** This distance is neither geographical, in the sense of having a clear perception of far and near, nor the distance of normal lifespace as in dialogue space. It is rather the mediated space-time in which all distances are made quasi-near. (I can hear you just about as well from the next town as from California or even Europe—if the technology is good), but equivalently you are never perceptually fully present and thus you remain simultaneously irreally distant. In short, the medium transforms the other and the situation in which the other is made present. This transformation, I shall say, is **non-neutral.**

So far, I have taken a familiar situation and begun to unravel its effects within what are for us normal experiences. Familiarity often covers over what may be noted to be quite striking effects. We do not think twice about telephones, yet they dramatically transform the possibility of human dialogue, both making it possible in situations never before available, and also making it possible by transforming the very meaning of the presence and location of the other.

What I have suggested concerning the telephone also bears its analogy to the initial example of sensory deprivation. The telephone is a mono-sense medium and thus is a partial sensory deprivation. But this deprivation is ambiguous. Its familiar mediation is such that we now have habitual patterns of telephone relations which we take for granted. There is currently much experimentation with an audio-visual form of communication, a television-phone. The ambiguity of our habit is pointed up by the mixed response to such a device—some think it would be nice to be able to see the other as well as talk to him or her, while others, on second thought, note that they might well be caught with hair in curlers or without their pajamas. There are both advantages and disadvantages to the "deprivation." This is to say that the telephone as a medium has been taken into daily life in a certain way. And we organize our very communication patterns around the peculiar capacities of instrumental embodiment. Such effects are subtle and precisely because they are so familiar, we may fail to take note of the way in which our very experience of the other has been transformed.

A more complex medium—let us take television—displays the same essential features. Although the television is bi-sensory (audio-visual) it remains both an extension of our sensory experience in space-time and a reduction of that experience. In this instance the transformation of space-time may be quite dramatic, so much so that the "live" performance is the exception to the general practice of replay in which the immediate lifeworld reference may no longer even exist. I only too well recall the somewhat ghoulish anti-cigarette commercial in which a recently dead actor had pre-taped his moral not to smoke. He indicated that he would be dead of lung cancer when seen on television. The television brings what was past and that which is or was elsewhere into the near-distance of the media **now**. In this sense it re-enforces our experience of an irreal presence of mediated otherness. The quasi-abstract character of the television image remains untouchable and distant while simultaneously being present here and now. But what stands forth as the focal phenomenon is the pervasive presence of the mediated now, the near-distance of what is heard and viewed.

The extension-reduction of media has another facet as well. In format, contemporary television (at least in capitalist countries) differentiates little between the 7 o'clock news and Walt Disney. A report on deaths in some world revolution could just as well be interrupted by a commercial as could segments of a cartoon feature. But the point here is not a diatribe against commercialism; it is rather the observation that space-time in the medium takes on a certain disjunctive character. The medium has as a capacity, a technological "transcendence," over ordinary space-time. The freedom of control possible in editing and constructing a program is closer to the revery, to the imaginative dimension than to ordinary life. (This is obviously not to extoll the current "imaginativeness" of television!) It has, therefore, the same tempting power as the more ancient medium, print, for those who wish to escape from tedium, boredom and the ordinary. The viewer may escape into the reproduced revery just as the reader of pulp novels may do.

I do not intend, in this characterization, to suggest that escape is the only possibility of media such as print or television--to the contrary, the extension which is possible to a wider world of humanity, nature, or whatever is also a possibility. What I am suggesting, however, is that the extension is of a particular kind, an extension which simultaneously reduces, amplifies and transforms the referant to some particular **mediated** presence.

The media world is thus a transformed world. Note that I am not saying that it is either merely an imitation of or reproduction of the ordinary perceptual world. But I am saying that it is a variant "world." So far the level of analysis has only varied between direct perceptual situations in which media occupy some position between the experiencer and the referent of the experience. However, there is a complication which enters this situation. The mediated perceptual situation remains in a basic sense perceptual. It is I who see the television; who hear the voices. And while the presumed ultimate referent is somewhere else, I also immediately perceive the television presence. This is to make the obvious point that all experience has its perceptually basic dimension (including the fully "sensory deprivation" experience), but it is also to point to something else. Insofar as the medium is immediately experienced, it also transforms the larger perceptual situation. Indeed, media become part of the total perceptual situation. And if at the first level one may detect the irreal dimension of a mediated perception, at a second level one can also claim that this mediation has now been materialized and thus becomes part of reality. This is, of course, to say that media have a "real" effect.

At this level the real effect of media has certain implications for the way in which we interpret our overall experience. I shall describe this effect by a series of gradations such that initial analogies which are taken to be metaphorical gradually become the common coin such that they are taken to be literal. For example, in much psychological description and certainly in that which records descriptions of experience by subjects, it is now common to describe imagination, memory, dreams and other image-related experience as "like" a movie. At this stage we have a clear example of cross-sorting in which there are obvious analogies between two distinctly different phenomena. What tends to get emphasized are, in fact, the similarities rather than the differences although the differences may well be as important as the similarities.

Such cross-sorting has often become so traditional that it becomes assumed that the likeness is virtually identical. In epistemology one may illustrate this by referring to the long and deeply held traditions which claim that imagination **reproduces** perception and is **isomorphic** with it, whereas this is simply phenomenologically false. (For example, the focal plane of visual imagination is quite distinct from that of perception in that it is "shallower." Furthermore, the relation and ratio of the core reference imaginatively is and can be radically different than in perception. In the imagined Pegasus the field within which it is located imaginatively can be so vague and indistinct as to mislead the imaginer into thinking there is no ground for the figure at all whereas perceptually while one can attempt to ignore the background, once pointed out it becomes obvious that there is no painted Pegasus except against a ground.)[2]

In the first cross-sorting approximation, the similarities are merely noted and distinctions glossed over. Life becomes "like" the movies just as movies may be life-like. (Many persons remark that it seems as if they have "seen this movie before" or report that they feel like they have "been in this movie before.")

Note that in this cross-sorting, causal relations or relations of origination may work in either direction. Certainly prior to the experience of movies and television, imagination and memory would not have been described as "movie-like." Rather, imaginers and rememberers inverted the process and often deliberately modelled their sequences upon imaginations and memories (as did literature before). But once having become part of the lifeworld, the dream-imagined-remembered sequences now materialized become part of the way in which we come to understand ourselves and our world.

At the other end of the process of cross-sorting in which a metaphorical relation becomes understood as non-metaphorical, one can also discern a relation to media induced experience. In recent years I have attended a number of interdisciplinary conferences dealing with computer technology and artificial intelligence. To my constant amazement I find that there are always a number of participants (usually mathematicians and highly theoretically oriented computer programmers) who take the human mind and the computer not to be metaphorically similar, but (potentially) literally identical. Here the process of cross-sorting has lost its suggestive analogical basis and become a metaphysics.[3] But this phenomenon should be expected by a phenomenologist. If it is the case that intentionality is genuinely interactive between world and self; and if that "world" increasingly becomes encapsulated or at least focused upon some narrow set of intriguing phenomena; then at least for the non-critical and reductively predisposed mind it becomes almost inevitable that "I" will become "like" my experienced "world."

I am suggesting that a technological world is not only one in which we are increasingly related to the media, but that such relations are non-neutral in at least two important senses. I have shown how the transformation of basic perceptual experience occurs in the experience of media; and now I have suggested that at the level of human self-interpretation the experience of media become pervasive and familiar and

2. Edward S. Casey, IMAGINING (Indiana University Press, 1976).

3. Herbert Dreyfus, WHAT COMPUTERS CAN'T DO (Harper and Row, 1972).

begin to inform our ways of understanding ourselves. While I suggest that this effect is pervasive and subtle (and it is not linear in that single items or developments would be hard, if not impossible, to detect), it is an effect which is hard to demonstrate globally.

Negatively, I am suggesting that media effects are not linear. While occasionally some specific violent act might be imitated in real life, such a linear effect is rare and probably absurd. But a global effect may occur and, while harder to demonstrate, can be suggested with reason. I shall develop such a speculation again along the lines of the phenomenoloigcal model I have been using.

First, I have noted that all mediated experience is an experience which varies from direct or unmediated experience in that what is experienced occurs in an irreal near-distance. Were this near-distance to become not only a familiar experience, but a frequently dominant one, then the development of a more or less permanent attitude might be developed as well. Such attitude I shall call **aesthetic** in a special sense.

An aesthetic stance is one which is between direct, pragmatic and actional involvement and a stance which is primarily contemplative, distancing and disinterested (the "observer attitude" attributed to science). Were such a stance to become standard, then one might well think of all spaces and times as equivalent and both quasi-near and quasi-far. Yet this is exactly the "world" which is portrayed to us through television and cinema. Distance to the far, to the past is reduced, but it stops short of the bite of immediately demanding reality.

Now what if this aesthetic stance or attitude were to be taken as the normal way in which we were to act, to relate, to behave? By reversing the perspective this way, one might then predict certain things about how human relationships might be considered, how action is to be undertaken, and how behavior would occur. Take intimate relationships as an example—what would an aesthetic stance imply in such a context? Near-distance might well imply something between absolute involvement and contemplative observation. It might imply enjoyable engagement, but stop short of permanent commitment. It might imply a certain interchangeability of relationships, an equivalence of types of relationships as the scene changes not only through such variations becoming familiar in daily life, but through the near-distance which allows enjoyable toleration. I probably need not push the point for one to see that at least one dimension of society "lives" in exactly such a mode. This is not a direct, but a possible indirect effect of a media conditioned attitude. And it is an effect which may be established apart from the content of programming in the media.

What is insidious in such television phenomena as "Soap" and "General Hospital" is not the humorous or the pathetic interchangeability of individuals nor the more or less resemblance which this interchangeability bears to much of actual life, as it is the establishment of these human affairs as a spectacle to be watched and enjoyed.

Although Shakespeare anticipated the world as stage, he could not have known that what was powerful metaphor might come close to being commonplace in a media saturated society. Might we not have become or yet become too much **like** our world, a world which we increasingly make through our media?

An Examination of the Concept
of Interaction Involvement
using Phenomenological
and Empirical Methods

Donald J. Cegala

My hold on the past and future is precarious, and my possession of my own time is always postponed until a stage when
I may fully understand it, yet this stage can never be
reached, since it would be one more moment, bounded by
the horizon of its future, and requiring in its turn further
developments in order to be understood.

M. Merleau-Ponty
Phenomenology of Perception

Merleau-Ponty's penetrating observation captures succinctly
the basic dilemma of attempting to understand completely any
experience. It is, therefore, with considerable trepidation
that I propose to address the question: **How is the experience
of interpersonal communication possible?** Following Merleau-
Ponty's wisdom, I do not propose to provide a complete
answer to the question. Instead, my goal is to identify what
seem to be necessary, though perhaps not sufficient, conditions for the experience of interpersonal communication. Even
so, this project is potentially rampant with ambiguity from
the outset, as there are multiple meanings for the term "interpersonal communication."

In this essay, interpersonal communication refers to contexts
where individuals interact dynamically, usually face to face,
although some mediated interactions such as conversations on
an intercomm or telephone also apply. The essence of interpersonal communication is that there is an immediacy of
speaker/listener role exchange among participants. Interpersonal communication contexts allow for, in fact demand, a
dynamic exchange of speaker/listener roles. In addition, this

INTERPERSONAL COMMUNICATION: Essays in Phenomenology and Hermeneutics,
ed., Joseph J. Pilotta, Copyright 1982, The Center for Advanced Research in
Phenomenology, Inc. and co-published by arrangement with The University Press
of America, Inc.

exchange centers on a topic(s) of conversation; that is, the interaction is focused.[1]

Having clarified the kind of communication of interest in this essay, the central question may again be addressed. To ask how interpersonal communication is possible is to imply a concern about intersubjectivity. How is it that two or more subjects can share experience with respect to a topic of conversation? What is necessary for such an experience? Responses to these questions are fundamental, yet complex. Intersubjectivity may be examined from several levels of experience.

At one level, intersubjectivity by definition is a function of two or more persons interacting in some way. Yet, at another level intersubjectivity may be examined from an individual point of view, concerned with what each person contributes to the experience of interpersonal communication. These levels of intersubjectivity seem to address different, but related, processes of interpersonal communication. It will be suggested here that the first level of intersubjectivity focuses on the establishment of the communicative relationship, while the second level speaks to the maintenance of this relationship. Both levels of intersubjectivity seem important to the central question of: How is interpersonal communication possible? At the same time, these aspects of intersubjectivity are inextricably linked to the most fundamental level of experience. It is at this level that the analysis begins.

The Intentionality of Consciousness

An analysis of interpersonal communication might begin by asking: How is it possible to recognize an object as human?[2] This is the most basic question of intersubjectivity, as it is concerned with how subject and non-subject are related in common experience. In short, how is it possible to experience anything? Clearly this question has been a central topic of Western philosophy for centuries and, of course, phenomenology's purpose was to rid all investigations of the dilemmas posed by how idealism and rationalism responded to the question. At this level of abstraction one's view of intersubjectivity has profound implications for a basic understanding of all experience, not just interpersonal communication. Central to this level of intersubjectivity is Edmund Husserl's concept of the intentionality of consciousness.

Descartes long ago made the telling observation "cogito ergo sum" (I think, therefore I am). The truly indubitable facticity

1. Erving Goffman, BEHAVIOR IN PUBLIC PLACES (Free Press, 1963).

2. See David W. Hamlyn, "Person-Perception and Our Understanding of Others," UNDERSTANDING OTHER PERSONS, ed. Theodore Mischel (Basil Blackwell, 1974).

of the lived-world is that we experience consciousness. However, unlike Descartes, Husserl did not separate the world into the conscious mind and that of which it is conscious. Instead, Husserl emphasized the intentionality of consciousness; that is to say, that consciousness is always directed toward some object, it always has content. One is always conscious of . . . (something). The interpretation of consciousness as intentional eliminates the possibility of viewing it as empty or closed upon itself. A world devoid of objects leaves nothing to be conscious of! Similarly, a world of reality that is unknowable is unthinkable. In brief, the intentional structure of consciousness posits a self-evident unity between the conscious mind and that of which it is conscious. Accordingly, humans' ability to recognize objects as human is self-evident from birth. We are by nature intentional beings and we recognize other humans as such.

The intentional structure of consciousness addresses the most fundamental question about how interpersonal communication is possible. However, the more practical implications of this structure are perhaps clarified by a focus on the term "communication."

Mutual Intentional Recognition

Robert Scott [3] has suggested that mutual intentionality recognition is critical to establishing parameters on the concept of communication. This notion seems especially relevant to face to face interaction, as it allows for a distinction between intentional beings **as observers** attributing meaning to others' behavior and intentional beings jointly creating meaning (i.e., interpersonal communication). Consider, for example, the situation in which an individual is unknowingly observed talking to his plants as he conducts his morning gardening routine. At this point the observer is attributing meaning to the gardener's behavior, perhaps wondering if he has gone crazy or has established some unique communication with plants. However, when the gardener notes that he is being observed, the meaning of the situation changes dramatically for both the gardener and observer. The point at which the observer's intentionality is recognized (and vice versa) establishes a relationship that goes beyond attributed meanings because the gardener and observer now must mutually relate to one another as subjects. The gardener, recognizing an intentional human agent, must now account for his own behavior in relation to that agent, perhaps feeling foolish cr angry for the intrusion. Similarly, the observer must also now account for his behavior

3. Robert L. Scott, "Communication As An Intentional, Social System," HUMAN COMMUNICATION RESEARCH, 3 (Spring, 1977), 258-268.

not as an observer, but as a subject recognized by another subject.

The point of this example is to underscore that something unique happens when humans recognize that they are the content of another's consciousness. Such recognition allows for the mutual exchange of human experiencing. For sure an observer and actor may be intersubjective in the sense that both share outer space and time; that is, space and time that can be objectively measured. However, mutual intentionality recognition allows for the possibility of sharing the lived experience [4] of time and space. As such, it seems to be at the very essence of interpersonal communication. Mutual intentionality recognition underscores that communication is fundamentally a social experience. It provides the ontological basis for what might be called "interpersonal intersubjectivity," that is, the mutual meeting of two subjects, as opposed to a subject and object.

The suggestion, then, is that mutual intentionality recognition is necessary for the establishment of the interpersonal communicative relationship. It marks the point where individuals may share the lived experience of time and space. Yet, it does only that. The communicative relationship may dissolve as quickly as it is established. Moreover, the dissolution of the relationship seems only partially dependent upon individuals' interaction, as an individual may break the relationship. There is the sense, then, that something is needed to maintain the communicative relationship. The necessary ingredient is implied in the nature of human intentionality.

Human intentionality is focused and shared through language. Once humans mutually recognize their intentionality, the communicative relationship must be maintained by sharing their respective intentionality foci through language. This means more than merely talking to one another. It involves a sharing of consciousness that is as subtle, yet pervasive, as mutual intentionality recognition.

Maintenance of the interpersonal communicative relationship demands that individuals have the meanings of self, other and situation as the dominant content of their consciousness. In other words, the individual must fully participate with the immediate, ongoing environment. Anything less than this full participation will result in removal or withdrawal from the interaction of which the individual is supposedly part.

It should be understood, however, that not all forms of withdrawal are detrimental to the communicative relationship. For

4. See Alfred Schutz, COLLECTED PAPERS II: Studies in Social Theory (The Hague, 1964).

example, contemplation prior to answering a question posed by one's interlocutor is a form of momentary withdrawal that may suggest considerable participation with the ongoing reality. Note, however, that in this instance, the communicative relationship is still the dominant content of the individual's consciousness, as the topic of conversation is the focus of his/ her contemplation. Compare this form of momentary withdrawal with a brief preoccupation about matters unrelated to a conversation (e.g., a thought about an undone task of importance). Clearly, the latter form of withdrawal results in a removal from the reality of the ongoing conversation. Furthermore, this removal is a break in intersubjectivity and is potentially detrimental to the interpersonal communicative relationship.

Of course, not all such breaks in intersubjectivity result in significant negative consequences; in fact, individuals seem quite adept at communicating in spite of such occurrences. However, they do seem to be problematic when a person characteristically engages in these breaks from intersubjectivity. Such behavior is the concern of interaction involvement.

Interaction Involvement

The preceding suggests that involvement in interaction is a second necessary condition for the experience of interpersonal communication. Such involvement results in taking another into account, as described by Blumer:

> Taking another person into account means more than merely being in his presence or merely responding to him. Two individuals asleep in a bed may respond to each other as they shift in their sleeping postures; however, they are not taking each other into account in such responses. Taking another person into account means being aware of him, identifying him in some way, making some judgment or appraisal of him, identifying the meaning of his action, trying to find out what he has on his mind or trying to figure out what he intends to do. Such awareness of another person in this sense of taking him and his acts into consideration becomes the occasion for orienting oneself and for the direction of one's own conduct. One takes the other person and his action into account not merely at the point of initial contact, but actually throughout the period of interaction. One has to keep abreast of the action of the other, noting what he says at this point and that point or interpreting his movements as they appear, one after another. Perceiving, defining and judging the other person and his action and organizing oneself in terms of such definitions and judgments constitute a continuing or running process.[5]

5. Herbert Blumer, "Psychological Import of the Human Group," GROUP RELATIONS AT THE CROSSROADS, eds. M. Sherif and M.O. Wilson (Harper and Brothers, 1953), p. 194.

This continuing process surely demands that the individual acquire an apprehension of the ongoing social reality of which he/she is supposedly part. Such apprehension demands a continuous participation with the social; that is, an ongoing integration of one's thoughts, feelings, and experiences with the moment to moment unfolding of conversation. Yet, it is clear that this process must be transparent to the act of communicating itself, or individuals would in effect remove themselves from the very interaction in which they were supposedly participating. The needed transparency is achieved by individuals' fundamental orientation toward social interaction. It is believed that the concept of interaction involvement is basic to this orientation.

Interaction involvement has been defined as the extent to to which an individual partakes in an immediate social environment.[6] One's interaction involvement is a function of two related processes--attentiveness and perceptiveness. Attentiveness is concerned with the extent to which individuals are cognizant of environmental cues, especially the interlocutor's behavior. Perceptiveness is the extent to which an individual is knowledgable of the meanings that others assign to one's own behavior and the meanings that one ought to assign to others' behavior. In brief, attentiveness speaks to how the individual directs his/her consciousness to the "outer" social world, while perceptiveness is the relative certainty that the individual has about the meaning of the immediate environment.

When highly involved, an individual is attentive and perceptive to the ongoing interaction, taking alter into account and assessing the evolving relationship between them. Alternatively, when individuals are low in interaction involvement they are at least partially removed psychologically from the ongoing interaction, often directing their attention to matters unrelated to the conversation. In effect, low involvement is a turning inward, a withdrawal from the other and ongoing interaction.

It has been suggested that momentary lows in involvement are not unusual or necessarily detrimental to interpersonal communication. However, when individuals have a characteristically low involvement orientation toward their interactions it

6. Donald J. Cegala, "Interaction Involvement: A Cognitive Dimension of Communicative Competence," COMMUNICATION EDUCATION, 30 (April, 1981); "The Role and Assessment of Prerequisite Behaviors in Communication Instruction," COMMUNICATION IN THE CLASSROOM: Contemporary Theory and Practice, ed. Larry L. Barker (Prentice-Hall, 1981); Donald J. Cegala and Grant T. Savage, "An Examination of Interaction Involvement and Selected Nonverbal Behavior," unpublished paper, 1981.

can be quite dysfunctional to the maintenance of interpersonal communication. The initial empirical research on interaction involvement has been designed to identify individuals' characteristic orientation toward interpersonal communication. This research has resulted in the development of a self report questionnaire. The interaction involvement scale has been used to gather data on approximately 1,500 individuals over the last several years. It has been demonstrated through factor analysis that the scale items cluster according to the hypothesized dimensions of attentiveness and perceptiveness.[7] While there are obvious weaknesses associated with self report questionnaires, the scale appears quite useful in predicting individuals' verbal and nonverbal behavior in conversational settings.

In one study high and low involvement individuals were paired in dyads and given the task of acquiring information of a personal nature from the dyad partner.[8] The expectation was that low involved people would perform less effectively on this task because they would be less able to direct the conversation in ways that would allow them to obtain the personal information without loss of face to self or other. This expectation was supported rather strongly. The resulting statistical prediction model (based on involvement scores) allowed 70 percent of the individuals to be correctly classified as successful or unsuccessful on the task. Perhaps more importantly, the transcripts of the interactions suggested that some low involved individuals missed opportunities to direct the conversation to their benefit, while others seemed to ignore the immediate topic of conversation and to change it abruptly in order to achieve their goal. These results suggest that low involved people were less plugged into the flow of interaction and, consequently, were less able to adapt to the demands of the situation.

Further evidence for the validity of the interaction involvement concept was found in patterns of individuals' nonverbal behavior.[9] In particular, low involved males were found to engage in less eye gaze while speaking and less direct eye contact than highly involved males. These results are consistent with several philosophical studies that suggest that eye gaze is a pervasive factor in establishing and maintaining intersubjectivity.[10]

7. See Cegala, "Interaction Involvement: A Cognitive Dimension of Communicative Competence."

8. Ibid.

9. Cegala and Savage, "An Examination of Interaction Involvement and Selected Nonverbal Behavior."

10. See John Heron, "The Phenomenology of Social Encounter: The Gaze," PHILOSOPHY AND PHENOMENOLOGICAL RESEARCH, 31 (December, 1970), 243-264; J-P. Sartre, BEING AND NOTHINGNESS, trans. H. Barnes (Rider, 1943).

Other nonverbal behaviors also may suggest relative degrees of intersubjectivity during communication. For example, Norbert Freedman [11] has conducted research on object and body focused gesturing, suggesting that when individuals engage in self touching (i.e., body focused) during interpersonal communication they are turning inward and have less intent to communicate. Alternatively, gesturing away from the body and toward one's communication partner (i.e., object focused) is thought to reflect an outward orientation and intent to communicate. Based on these findings, we expected to observe more body focused gesturing among lowly involved individuals and more object focused gesturing among highly involved people. The results in general supported expectations, except that they were complicated by an apparent sex difference in the meaning and function of these gestures.[12] In particular, they were found to reflect different levels of emotionality in males and females. This result has directed current research to focus on the relationship between interaction involvement and emotionality. Preliminary findings suggest that individuals who characteristically assume a low involvement orientation also tend to be highly emotional. This observation is consistent with other work on the nature of mood and intersubjectivity. For example, Heidegger [13] suggests that mood is a primary disclosure of being-in-the-world, thus indicating that it is relevant to what may or may not be realized by the individual. For Heidegger, mood clearly plays a significant role in one's intersubjectivity. A similar conclusion may be reached by examining the history of work on human temperament [14] and more recent empirical research on personality.[15]

Although interpersonal communication by definition is a function of the interaction among individuals, each person contributes to the maintenance of the communicative relationship in part by his/her orientation to the communicative act itself. Too often empirical research on interpersonal communication has neglected the role of such individual differences in favor of research models that stress mean tendencies across individuals.

11. Norbert Freedman, "The Analysis of Movement Behavior During the Clinical Interview," STUDIES IN DYADIC COMMUNICATION, eds. Aron Wolfe Siegman and Benjamin Pope (Pergamon Press, 1972).

12. See Cegala and Savage.

13. Martin Heidegger, BEING AND TIME, trans. John Macquarrie and Edward Robinson (Harper & Row, 1962).

14. See Abraham A. Roback, THE PSYCHOLOGY OF CHARACTER (Harcourt, Brace & Company, 1927).

15. Hans J. Eysenck, THE BIOLOGICAL BASIS OF PERSONALITY (Charles C. Thomas, 1967); Hans J. Eysenck and Sybil B.G. Eysenck, PERSONALITY STRUCTURE AND MEASUREMENT (Routledge & Kegan Paul, 1969).

While such an approach is useful, ultimately most applications of communication research are concerned with the individual level of behavior. The program of research on interaction involvement is designed to address this concern.

Postscript

This essay began with the question: What makes the experience of interpersonal communication possible? **The response has been mutual intentionality recognition and interaction involvement.** These seem to be necessary for the establishment and maintenance of interpersonal communication.

It is perhaps evident that my primary interest in this project lies with the concept of interaction involvement. Until now the published research on involvement has been grounded in the positivist tradition, the approach I was socialized into as a graduate student in communication. The invitation to write about interaction involvement for this collection has given me an opportunity to delineate the philosophical basis from which the concept was derived. It is hoped that this statement has illustrated a way in which the methods and interests of normal social science and phenomenology can be integrated in a useful fashion. Although attempts to integrate differing schools of thought often wind up alienating everyone, it is hoped that such has not happened here. It is believed that far more is to be gained by attempts to integrate these schools of thought than is likely to occur from their separation.

Contexts for Communication:
An Introduction
to the Contribution
of Jean Gebser

Elizabeth A. Behnke

When Alfred Schutz turned to the experience of "making music together" as a clue for one of the fundamental conditions for communication in general,[1] he gave us a theme still being varied and developed today. The "mutual tuning-in relationship" presupposed for all possible communication is less an unequivocal discovery on his part than an invitation to further clarification and exemplification. We might ask, for example, just what this mutual tuning-in might consist of; and we might use the musical metaphor to formulate other leading questions about the communication process. For example, what are the tacit principles of voice-leading governing our counterpoint? What are the temporal structures of our melodies? What vectors and valences in our harmonic system silently determine the consonances and dissonances of our encounter? What repertoire of formal structures have we developed? And what are the unwritten conventions of our performance practice? In short: what is the pattern of assumptions supporting and shaping the style of our mutual improvisation?

Like the opening phrase of a musical score, such a question invites a response that prolongs rather than ends the dialogue--for if the opening motif could be definitively "answered" by the very next phrase, there would be little reason to develop the theme. It is part of music's structure that the opening notes presage a realm of implications whose possibilities are not exhausted in advance. Following the lead of the musical metaphor, then, I shall not attempt to furnish an

INTERPERSONAL COMMUNICATION: Essays in Phenomenology and Hermeneutics, ed., Joseph J. Pilotta, Copyright 1982, The Center for Advanced Research in Phenomenology, Inc. and co-published by arrangement with The University Press of America, Inc.

1. Alfred Schutz, "Making Music Together: A Study in Social Relationship," in his COLLECTED PAPERS, II: Studies in Social Theory, ed. Arvid Brodersen (Martinus Nijhoff, 1964), 159-78.

immediate "answer" to the questions I have chosen to open with. Instead, I shall try to sketch out the methodology required to respond to the realm they open.

The methodological context I propose incorporates strategies and assumptions drawn from four different sources; phenomenology, hermeneutics, dimensional understanding, and Gebserian world-thinking. For purposes of exposition, I shall discuss these working approaches in separate sections. In practice, however, they are intertwined. Though individual researchers may emphasize one or another strand in this web, or supplement the strategies I outline with insights from other sources, the methodological horizon I am attempting to present is meant as a coherent whole. For this reason, the reader is asked to suspend judgment until all its major theses have been articulated and some possible applications to the interpersonal communication field have been indicated.

Phenomenology

I shall begin with the guiding assumption that human beings are experiencing beings whose experience of nature, society, self, and one another consists of the experience of sense or meaning. Taken phenomenologically, "experience" may be defined as the "appearing" or simply "being given" of anything whatsoever, in whatever way. Phenomenologists "make no assumptions about what is or is not real"[2]—they accept whatever phenomena they or anyone else may encounter, attempting to articulate **how** such phenomena "make sense." Hence phenomena excluded by other traditions or methods (e.g., on the grounds that "such a thing cannot be measured," "it does not really exist," etc.) are valid areas for phenomenological investigation.

Phenomenological investigations as a whole have revealed that meaning does not arise haphazardly or arbitrarily, but is organized according to certain fundamental conditions. The world and experience are structured; they are bearers of sense in certain determinable ways. Such structures are manifest in linguistic habits, in works of art, in religious practices, in explicit and implicit laws and rules of behavior, in the socio-political organization of life, and so forth. The ways in which the world makes sense profoundly influence our understanding of the world. Yet these ways themselves tend to remain an unnoticed background. The very sense-making process, the "how" of experience, the structures through which things and events are "given," the tacit styles and textures

2. David Stewart and Algis Mickunas, EXPLORING PHENOMENOLOGY: A Guide to the Field and its Literature (American Library Association, 1974), p. 4.

of our awareness--these tend to efface themselves in favor of what is being experienced. Caught up in the commerce of everyday life, we experience meaning without asking how this is so.

Phenomenology, however, seeks to display the unnoticed process of structuring the world, elucidating the tacit "conditions" that are overlooked in our everyday attention to the world. Hence phenomenological analysis is primarily a shift of focus attempting to exhibit the sense-making process itself through the analysis of the conditions for a particular experience of meaning.

Though phenomenology highlights the conditions for experience--speaking, perhaps, of the "structures of consciousness" necessary for a particular phenomenon to appear in a particular way--it does not lose sight of a fundamental link between these conditions and the experienced phenomena. In what Don Ihde has called the "tribal language" of phenomenology, this link is referred to as the noetic-noematic correlation. We may translate or paraphrase this technical phrase by saying that what we have called "experience" is the joint, the hinge, the articulation wherein world and consciousness [3] mutually conspire in the event of "meaning"--be this meaning abstract or concrete, intellectual or sensual, private or public, inchoate or lucid.

Another technical term, "intentionality," is also used to refer to the relation between the process of experience and that which is experienced. "One way this is frequently put is that consciousness is consciousness of . . . (the ellipsis here indicating any possible object of consciousness)."[4] The intentional relation is not causal, as though some object impinged upon a thing called consciousness and caused it to "have an experience." Nor does it name an activity undertaken "on purpose" by a subject, as the everyday use of the adverb "intentionally" might lead us to suspect. Rather, it is another way of expressing the thesis that "objects of consciousness" and "subjects of consciousness" both presume a more fundamental sense-making process toward which phenomenology is directed. Finally, intentionality in the phenomenological sense is not solely a cognitive relation, the intentional relation is manifested in many modes of human experience.[5]

3. Phenomenology and related approaches have come to take the term "consciousness" in a broad sense, including but not limiting themselves to the notion of consciousness as the reflective awareness obtained in introspection.

4. Stewart and Mickunas, p. 8.

5. On this point, see, for example, Dorion Cairns, "The Many Senses and Denotations of the Word **Bewusstsein** ('Consciousness') in Edmund Husserl's Writings," in LIFE-WORLD AND CONSCIOUSNESS: Essays for Aron Gurwitsch, ed. Lester E. Embree (Northwestern University Press, 1972), especially pp. 27-29, and Georges Thinès, PHENOMENOLOGY AND THE SCIENCE OF BEHAVIOUR: An Historical and Epistemological approach (George Allen & Unwin, 1977), p. 141.

I shall return to the "fundamental conditions" of this sense-making process in another section. Before proceeding further, however, it is necessary to consider one mor key term in phenomenology: the notion of **epoché**. This Greek word means "abstention," as in a "suspension of judgment."[6] What are we asked to abstain from? From the assumptions we hold, implicitly or explicitly, about the nature of reality; from the explanations we automatically invoke, be they physical, psychological, etc.; from the presuppositions we may have absorbed from current philosophies and ideologies; from any conceptual grid we may uncritically employ to categorize lived experience; in short, from anything that intervenes between the open consciousness and "the things themselves." In a famous passage from the Preface to **Phenomenology of Perception**, Merleau-Ponty writes:

> It is because we are through and through compounded of relationships with the world that for us the only way to become aware of the fact is to suspend the resultant activity, to refuse it our complicity . . . or yet again, to put it "out of play." Not because we reject the certainties of common sense and a natural attitude to things . . . but because, being the presupposed basis of any thought . . . they are taken for granted, and go unnoticed, and because in order to arouse them and bring them to view, we have to suspend for a moment our recognition of them.[7]

If in some way we can learn the knack of extricating ourselves from the unnoticed background of experience, we are free to describe what is essential to it; we can begin to see it for what it is.

There is much more to phenomenology than the elements I have chosen to present here. But the problem of actually unhinging ourselves from the taken-for-granted structures of experience already leads toward hermeneutics, and it is to this discipline that I shall now turn.

Hermeneutics

The study of hermeneutics alone might be considered a fertile source of tools and concepts for the field of communication, for hermeneutics, in its many branches, has been concerned with the communication of meaning through texts and their interpretation.[8] However, even though hermeneutics is often

6. For a discussion of this and related phenomenological terminology, see Stewart and Mickunas, pp. 7, 26-27.

7. Maurice Merleau-Ponty, PHENOMENOLOGY OF PERCEPTION, trans. Colin Smith (Routledge & Kegan Paul, 1962), p. xiii.

8. For a survey of relevant publications, see Thomas M. Seebohm, "The Problem of Hermeneutics in Recent Anglo-American Literature," PHILOSOPHY AND RHETORIC, 10 (1977), 180-98, 263-75.

associated with text interpretation, it may also be directed toward human existence itself.

Wilhelm Dilthey (1833-1911) was evidently the first to begin "to see in hermeneutics the foundation for the **Geisteswissenschaften**--that is, all the humanities and social sciences, all those disciplines which interpret expressions of man's inner life whether the expressions be gestures, historical actions, codified law, art works, or literature."[9] Prior to Dilthey, the notion of hermeneutics was most closely associated with exegesis; one of its influential contributions was the application of grammatical and philological analysis to biblical texts in an effort to understand them in their historical context and to interpret their continuing meaning for our time. The term "hermeneutics" may still properly be used with reference to the problem of interpreting, say, a difficult passage in a received text. But in the twentieth century it has gradually enlarged both its field of application and its methodological repertoire. The works of Heidegger have been crucial in developing the wider sense of the term. For Heidegger, the human's temporal structure is constitutive of his or her very being. Thus the attempt to interpret and to understand human being in terms of an existential and historical context may properly be called a hermeneutical endeavor. [10] Such an approach may appropriate the strategies of phenomenology in order to decipher the meaning of our pre-philosophical insertion in the world, resulting in what has been called "phenomenological hermeneutics."

It seems at first as though it is phenomenology that has come to the rescue of hermeneutics, lending it a methodological orientation within which the tacit dimensions of the life-world (**Lebenswelt**) may first emerge in order to be interpreted. But phenomenology itself had made an ambitious claim in its project of becoming a philosophy without presuppositions. From the point of view of hermeneutics, this is a misleading goal, for every phenomenological interpretation already begins from within a historical, cultural, and linguistic context. As individuals, we may find it easy to set certain prejudices aside and to place certain favorite theories out of play. But the very language we use to carry on the investigation functions as a pre-personal, anonymous "habitat" influencing perception as well as thought. Pervaded with leading

9. Richard E. Palmer, HERMENEUTICS: Interpretation Theory in Schleiermacher, Dilthey, Heidegger, and Gadamer (Northwestern University Press, 1969), p. 98.

10. Richard M. Zaner, "**Eidos** and Science," in PHENOMENOLOGY AND THE SOCIAL SCIENCES: A Dialogue, ed. Joseph Bien (Martinus Nijhoff, 1978), pp. 1-19.

metaphors, polarized by its own syntax, and admitting of
certain distinctions but not others, this obligatory linguistic
context marks us as participants in a particular tradition.
Even if we recognize a perception not mediated by language,
this perception can be shown to be a function of culture. We
are ineluctably wedded to our situation, and the **epoché** seems
out of reach.

This becomes particularly clear when we are concerned with
other cultural traditions--or even with interpreting past phases
of our own traditions. As researchers, we are not immune from
the proclivities of our own culture; we are not worldless, but
rooted in the concrete life-world of a particular civilization.
How are we to get clear of the "hidden dimensions" of our
context; how can we escape the "deep structure" silently
shaping even our attempts to frame the question of escape?

The researcher's predicament rests on a conception of the
epoché as a pure transparency, a complete renunciation of
every conceivable--and inconceivable--presupposition, affording
immediate access to whatever it is that must be interpreted.
But the interpreter (and the act of interpretation itself) cannot be allowed to vanish in this way. What is needed is a
self-hermeneutics that permits the researcher to become diaphanously aware of his or her own tacit sense-making processes while these processes are still in operation. If we use
the metaphor of a lens to describe the cultural and historical
context that inevitably configures our vision (and our
language), we may conceive of the phenomenological **epoché**
as a way of taking into account the curvature of our own lens,
diaphanously seeing our index of refraction for what it is
while simultaneously seeing through it toward the field on
which it is trained. Although I shall continue to set aside
any presupposition of the reality of some "undistorted" vista
upon which all such lenses are focused, it should at least
be possible to begin compensating for the calibration of our
own lens. And perhaps we may learn to adjust it, to shift
our style of focusing in accordance with the interpretative
context.

But this is only possible if we have a broad enough
methodological horizon. What is required is a background
identity against which various historical and cultural contexts
might be profiled: some "common denominators" in terms of
which the similarity and diversity of the fundamental conditions for experience in each context may be understood.
Dimensional understanding may be called upon to fill this
role.

Dimensional Understanding

Systematic reflection on experience has led certain phenomenologists, particularly Husserl, to the insight that experience is structured in terms of certain "fundamental conditions": time and space. These two conditions—which Husserl considered elemental components—and others to be mentioned below may be called basic dimensions of experience. Dimensional understanding makes no claim to be a mathematical strategy. But I shall turn to a simple mathematical example in order to clarify this use of the term.

Mathematicians use the term "dimension" to refer to the range of each of the independent coordinates necessary to specify information about a given point or event. Though not all mathematical dimensions may be as easily diagrammed, it is convenient here to think of the Cartesian coordinates (x and y). These rectilinear axes define a familiar two-dimensional scheme. Points in the system may be described with reference to both the available dimensions; the coordinates express the location of specific points in terms of the background frame of reference these axes set up. Though individual points may vary in location, the two dimensions in this example function as invariants—as identitites with respect to which the differing locations are both perceived and expressed. Yet these invariants themselves cannot be "located" by a similar description. We cannot measure how far they are from themselves, or where they are in terms of themselves, for they are "already there"; we have already assumed them as a prior horizon of investigation. The dimensions, in short, cannot be reduced to the status of the points whose descriptive context they provide.

It is likewise with the basic dimensions of experience. Space and time cannot be reduced to the status of the subjects and objects whose context they provide; therefore, these world-dimensions themselves cannot be adequately approached from the perspective of subjectivity or the perspective of objectivity. Traditional epistemology assumes a realm of subjectivity and one of objectivity, and then is constrained to place everything in either one or the other of these two domains. Dimensions such as space and time might at first be thought to supply a middle ground between the two, naming, for example, ways in which objects appear to and for subjects. But dimensional understanding is not an attempt to explain some mechanism mediating between these two regions. It is rather a way of understanding a tacit background that is prior to the subjective-objective distinction, and indeed, to the distinction between world and consciousness.[11]

Recall the phenomenological notion of experience as experience of "meaning." A dimensional understanding of meaning would "place" it with reference to the basic dimensions of experience. But note that given the phenomenological noetic-noematic correlation, these may be called **world-dimensions** as well as dimensions of experience. "World" and "consciousness" are correlative, and are mutually structured through the articulation of world-dimensions. In other words, consciousness—which is "consciousness of . . . "—is to be described in terms of the tacit conditions governing the sense-making process, i.e., in terms of a particular articulation of world-dimensions. Yet at the same time this account yields a description of the tacit background to be called "world."

Here "world" means neither an inventory of entities, objects, institutions, etc., nor an ideal unity posited by a subject. Furthermore, world is neither an illusion nor a necessarily approximate version of a "more real" reality. World "is" neither thing nor idea; it neither has, nor requires, any ontological status whatsoever, since the question of its "existence" or "reality" is set out of play. Definition by negation, however, is hardly satisfying. I shall therefore venture a provisional definition in positive terms: by "world" I mean a dimensional contexture operating as a tacit background of experience within a given culture or broad cultural tradition (see next section). The word "tacit" indicates that world functions as the requisite context whether or not we explicitly reflect on it. And the phrase "dimensional contexture" indicates that the world-context may be understood as a network of intertwined world-dimensions."[12] So far, I have mentioned only time and space. Movement may be added as well.[13] I have also chosen to approach corporeality as a world-dimension.[14]

But the methodological turn to such dimensions would be of little help if their articulation in human experience displayed no discernible pattern. It is the achievement of Jean Gebser

11. Cf. Eugen Fink, ZUR ONTOLOGISCHEN FRUEGESCHICHTE VON RAUM-ZEIT-BEWEGUNG (Martinus Nijhoff, 1957), pp. 31ff.

12. On the notion of contexture, see Richard M. Zaner, THE CONTEXT OF SELF: A Phenomenological Inquiry Using Medicine as a Clue (Ohio University Press, 1981), chapters 4 and 5.

13. See Algis Mickunas, "The Primacy of Movement," MAIN CURRENTS, 31 (1974), 8-12.

14. Elizabeth A. Behnke, "Integral Corporeality: Michael Murphy's JACOB ATABET and the Context of Transformation," International Association for Philosophy and Literature, Binghamton, New York, 10 May 1979.

to have recognized and described reoccuring patterns deline-
ating five basic worlds or dimensional contextures. Through
his pioneering labor, a seemingly abstract approach may be
applied to a multitude of concrete situations. His indispensable
contribution to the methodological horizon I am proposing will
be sketched in the next section.

Jean Gebser's Contribution

In his major work, **Ursprung und Gegenwart** (1949/53), Jean
Gebser (1905-1973) presents the following fundamental
"structures": the archaic, magic, mythic, mental, and integral
worlds.[15] His descriptions are supported by a wealth of evidence from many different cultures, and I shall not attempt
to duplicate that material here. My aim is simply to indicate
some of the range and depth of his work through condensed
"portraits" of the contextures he describes.

A word of caution is in order before beginning: expository
prose requires that we arrange what we have to say in linear
fashion, presenting topics one after the other. However, the
dimensional contextures introduced here should not be equated
with a historical progression across linear time; nor should
they be considered a "vertical" progression out of "lower"
levels into "higher" ones. Structures that may seem "earlier"
are not obsolete, but remain viable modes of experience in
our times. Indeed, it is crucial that we understand and integrate these possibilities. It follows that these world-contexts
are not mutually exclusive, but may be treated as co-present,
co-functioning contextures influencing and accommodating one
another. I must nevertheless begin somewhere with the
exposition, despite the danger that the Gebserian structures
might be misinterpreted as progressive stages in simple lineal
evolution (a thesis Gebser himself deliberately sets aside,
though he refers to radical contextural shifts with the phrase
"mutations of consciousness").

The archaic world is one of complete identity. Human and
cosmos are in no way distinct; the human being is so much
"one" with the surrounding world that there is not even any
consciousness of this identity, for such an awareness would
already require a separation between them. References to this
primordial contexture have been found in ancient descriptions
of paradise. Gebser's term "archaic" derives from the Greek
archē, "origin." For Gebser, this is not some temporal
beginning, no matter how primal, but an elemental and ever-
present ground. Thus the archaic contexture is "primordial"

---

15. Jean Gebser, ORIGINAL PRESENCE, trans. Algis Mickunas and Noel Berstad
(Ohio University Press, forthcoming).

in that it is radically ab–original. Space and time are not present in this dreamless world. Nevertheless, Gebser refers to this structure as pre–spatial and pre–temporal, in order to indicate that these world–dimensions provide the methodological background for his descriptions.

It is with the magic world that Gebser begins to speak of "unity" rather than "identity." The human is intertwined with nature, yet is aware of this vital interconnection, and responds with attempts to master nature through magic ritual. The magic contexture displays a fundamental interchangeability and transformability. Each thing, event, or entity may with equal validity be substituted for any other; a part may legitimately replace the whole (or the whole a part); each spatial or temporal point may assume the sense and significance of any other point. Hence space and time as we know them simply do not operate in the magic context. It is effectively spaceless and timeless, characterized not by a causal nexus, but by an immediate and vital sympathy among all creatures, things, and actions. Everything has **mana**: power is dispersed throughout the world rather than deployed solely by a human ego. The human does not face this world, but merges with it even while making magic in an attempt to extricate human projects from their enmeshment in nature. In the magic world, the human is egoless; it is the clan or the group, rather than the individual, that is pre–eminent. (We still feel this today on those occasions when a collection of individuals is forged into a single group, throbbing to a single beat, pervaded by a single emotion.) Consciousness is not an activity or function located "in" a self, but is a group sense based upon the interwovenness of all participants with their global situation; analogical and associative thinking predominate, and telepathy is not a mysterious or "paranormal" phenomenon, but an expression of this shared vital nexus.

The mythic contexture is the tacit background for the emergence of self as psyche. Humans begin to be aware of their inner experience, though family and community are still more important than the individual, and myth mirrors the inner mysteries of the soul. Neither enmeshed in the world nor facing it as an objective reality, the human swings in polar relationship with nature. Polarities (such as yin and yang, female and male) shape experience in general, functioning as the living symbols and images to which the human is psychically (psychologically) attuned. Spatial relations are depicted non-perspectivally; time is circular rather than linear, and human experience is articulated according to its cyclical rhythm. The dark, mysterious mother principle––**mater, matter, earth**––is more venerated than exploited. Intuitive and imaginative thinking, along with other qualities sometimes categorized as "feminine" (e.g., receptivity), play an important role. Familiar to us from depth psychology as well as from certain oriental philosophies, the mythic contexture easily exemplifies the notion that the world-contexts that Gebser describes are present possibilities to be integreated rather than "evolutionary stages" to be transcended.

The mental world and consciousness is structured in terms of three-dimensional space and unidirectional linear time—the "reality" we tacitly assume in modern technological civilizations. Mind begins to impose control over matter and psyche; social organization is dominated by the masculine, patriarchal principle. Man (for so we must now call the human) becomes aware of his body as the carrier of the self, and of the self as a unique historical individual. He thereby develops ego-consciousness and interprets experience as the direction of a subjective perspective upon an objective world. But at the same time, he introduces a fundamental dualism between an external world and a spatialized self. Opposition rather than polarity is the key to their relationship. The world is understood as being composed of objects confronting subjects who possess rational, calculative, purposive, and quantitative methods for the knowledge and appropriation of these objects. When this orientation is rigidly adhered to, the world becomes material, atomistic, and fragmented, and man is reduced to one more object to be manipulated. The ability to gain distance from the phenomena, to direct one's thinking according to logical principles, to develop clear and distinct ideas, to analyze experience in terms of causal relationships—all these are salient features of the mental contexture, and they represent powerful possibilities in human awareness. However, when the vital and psychic elements are continually suppressed in favor of a completely rational attitude, man becomes an alienated individual in an abstract world. And no amount of purely technological progress can make this world whole and meaningful again.

With the integral context, "space" is understood as space-time. Contemporary works of art may depict space aperspectivally: the vantage point of a single ego at a single now-point is no longer automatically assumed, as is the case with a strictly perspectival painting, and a global view is possible. Time plays a further integrative role: past and future are not mutually exclusive regions on a time line, but are gathered in a concrete presence that displays both past and future possibilities as part of the depth of the present. The word "time" itself no longer refers to a physical time "extended" across a spatialized succession of now-points, but names an intensifying, presencing power—an open, "four-dimensional" nexus or field accepting and calling for an integral consciousness as its correlate. Experience is no longer "impaled on the now-point" or limited to a single "perspective"; the integral consciousness is not only "ego-free" and "space-free," but also "time-free," i.e., liberated from the exclusive validity of a unidirectional, linear time composed of mutually exclusive now-moments. Thus it is that we may integrate, rather than "transcend" or "surpass," other dimensional contextures, even though they might seem to belong to "past" cultures. Such an integration does not connote the "compulsory unification" of disparate aspects into a single concept. Nor may it be identified with a synthesis always threatened by the opposition of a new antithesis. It might better be phrased as a "both/and" structure characterized by the co-presence of mutually diaphanous contexts.[16]

Diaphaneity (transparency) is evidently a fundamental element of experience in the integral world. No contexture is allowed to dominate or obscure the others; assuming a primarily mental orientation in one situation does not "block our vision" or blind us to the living presence of vital sympathy and psychic attunement. On the other hand, magic or mythic contexture may be assumed when appropriate without plunging us into an "irrational" darkness. And each of these structures must be diaphanously understood for what it is in order that we do not inadvertently rigidify it and thereby lose other possibilities. The integral world and consciousness-structure is holistic, incorporating not only the possibility of a homeostatic balance between other contextures, but also something more: an a-rational and global awareness yielding a qualitative transformation of experience. And for Gebser, as we have already mentioned, such a consciousness is correlative to the world it assumes and indicates: an open world, in its wholeness and depth.

Gebserian world-thinking is itself a powerful methodological context, even when its relationship to the other strategies I have presented is not emphasized. The foundational implications of his descriptions offer many possibilities for application in the communication field, some of which are suggested below.

---

16. The "both/and" formulation may also be expressed as a "neither/nor." Consider, for example, 20th century answers to the question: Is light a wave or a particle? The way the question is put assumes the "either-or" dualism characteristic of the mental contexture, and whether we reply with a "both/and" phrasing or with a "neither/nor" formulation, our answer will be qualitatively different: it will assume a different structure of consciousness.

Selected Applications in Interpersonal Communication Theory

I shall begin by identifying the background context tacitly informing a familiar communication model, presented here in truncated fashion for the sake of clarity. According to this model, a rational "message," represented in a form that we can analyze (and, ideally, measure) is purposively directed from "sender" to "receiver." I, the sender, put my thought into words in order to communicate it to you, the receiver, and though my subjective perspective will never be the same as yours, you will grasp what I'm trying to say if I have used language correctly. The assumed presence of an objective reality against which we can test our statements helps each of us gauge the meaning represented in the words of the other. Already, without further elaboration or refinement, this model exhibits hallmarks of the mental-rational contexture. Rather than prolong the discussion, I shall immediately juxtapose this model to another.

In the second model, communication rests upon receptivity and attunement. I must be open to the Other; he or she is not to be taken as an object confronting me, but as a Thou with whom I enter into polar relationship. For some writers, this relationship is expressed by silence—not a silence defined by the absence of auditory stimuli, but a deeper symbolic silence that is the ground of being on which communication rests. In this model, "silence is nothing less than the unifying mystery of our existence as linguistic beings."[17] The notions of polarity and mystery, as well as the stress upon symbol and attunement, indicate that the mythic contexture is assumed as a tacit background for this model. Such a model might be particularly appropriate for interpreting psychological aspects of communication.

Let us now turn the process around: rather than citing an existing model and then relating it to one of Gebser's fundamental contexts, I shall consider the magic contexture as the source of a model that might help interpret existing research in communication. As I have mentioned, the magic world is pervaded with the vital nexus—a sympathetic interwovenness of vital processes. W.S. Condon and W.D. Ogston have located such a vital sympathy linking participants in a conversation. While searching for "units" of behavior—a quest typical of the mental contexture—these researchers discovered that behavior could more aptly be described as

17. Nancy Jay Crumbine, "On Silence," HUMANITAS, 11 (1975), 164-65; cf. Bernard P. Dauenhauer, "On Silence," RESEARCH IN PHENOMENOLOGY, 3 (1973), 18-23, 26-27.

"a flowing and emergent pattern of configurations of change."[18] Through microanalysis of filmed conversations, they found that "the body of the speaker dances in time with his speech. Further, the body of the listener dances in rhythm with that of the speaker!"[19] The "dance" persists regardless of the psychological state of the participants or the rational content of their speech; it proceeds as inevitably as our other vital processes, and with as little conscious control. "Thus it is only a limited portion of communication which can be conceived of in terms of the model of messages sent and received."[20] This is an excellent example of how various contextures may be co-present, co-functioning elements of human experience. The researchers' own comments on the problems of interpreting data gleaned from detailed film analysis are illuminating:

> We live in a familiar, cognitive world which conveys some assurance about object and event boundaries; this also provides a context in terms of which we are often led to make our investigative distinctions. One becomes less confident of these familiar modes of dividing the stream of events when one faces the task of **inductively** establishing such boundaries. . . . The history of the present research indicates that what may be random from one perspective is often not random from a different perspective.[21]

The seemingly irrelevant micro-movements disclosed by the investigation may be meaningless in a mental-rational context. But their synchrony becomes highly significant when interpreted as a manifestation of the vital nexus, and admirably fleshes out Schutz's notion of a "mutual tuning-in relationship."

If is difficult at this juncture to suggest concrete applications of the Gebserian notion of the archaic structure. One might, however, speculate that the radical disintegration of all communicative processes might be related, not merely to a breakdown in certain psycho-physiological functions, but to the loss of a fundamental tacit "connection" with existence—an identity so deep we can hardly conceive it, and seldom experience it directly, except in its unaccountable

---

18. W.S. Condon and W.D. Ogston, "A Segmentation of Behavior," JOURNAL OF PSYCHIATRIC RESEARCH, 5 (1967), 224.

19. W.S. Condon and W.D. Ogston, "Sound Film Analysis of Normal and Pathological Behavior Patterns," JOURNAL OF NERVOUS AND MENTAL DISEASES, 143 (1966), 338.

20. William S. Condon, "Multiple Response to Sound in Dysfunctional Children," JOURNAL OF AUTISM AND CHILDHOOD SCHIZOPHRENIA, 5 (1975), 43. As this article indicates, the micro-dance, like other vital processes, may suffer pathological disruption.

21. Condon and Ogston (1967), pp. 229, 232.

absence.

Finally, I shall briefly indicate two ways in which the integral contexture may inform communication theory. (1) The integral world is a holistic context integrating the various textures and styles of awareness and "reality" outlined above. With this contexture, an individual is not bound to a single mode or model of communication. Different contextures may be appropriately swung into play as the occasion demands. Such communication exchanges might therefore be described as honoring tacit contracts between participants—contracts that specify which contexture is to be assumed as the tacit background for the exchange. With one friend, for example, I may find it prudent to operate in the mental-rational mode. Here we tacitly agree to say explicitly what we mean; I avoid trying to "read the other's mind," and perhaps re-state what I think he or she has just said to see if I've got the message he or she is trying to get across. With another friend, however, I may feel more comfortable when we have established an attunement where what we say is less important than the tone of voice in which we say it; where my gesture may mirror my friend's deepest feelings, and vice versa; where we become "soul-mates" in the mystery of the I-Thou encounter. In yet another situation, I may cultivate "telepathic" rapport with my partner. (The vital context is particularly appropriate for group improvisations among musicians and dancers—we move as one, without pre-arrangement, trusting our group sense—and for team sports.) Or I may manifest the magic contexture by weaving a dialogue of analogies and associations. In any case, communication in the integral contexture resists rigidification into a single model; and more than one model may be "true."

(2) The notion of integral awareness has yet another sort of implication for the study of communication, especially for participant-observation research. Contemporary investigations of the tacit background of experience are sometimes referred to as attempts to "see it for what it is." Within the mental-rational context, this would imply that we have gained a vantage pont "outside the system," a perspective from which this system may be viewed objectively in order that we may enumerate its characteristics. Gebser's work, however, suggests that the pattern "subject taking a perspective on an object" is itself characteristic of one context among others. And shifting to the integral mode does not grant us some further standpoint from which to prepare an "objective" description of other contexts, for we have not left them behind; they are not "objects," but dimensional contextures integrally present in our own tacit background as living possibilities. The problem is therefore not to avoid them, but to remain

aware of them even as they shape our experience. An integral understanding does not demand a release from the tacit conditions of experience; it makes them diaphanous from within. It respects lived experience in its wholeness, elucidating its articulations and articulating its meanings without severing the knower from the known. The approach presented in preceding sections has attempted to demonstrate the methodological requirements for such a claim.

Recapitulation of the Opening Theme

Schutz's description of the "mutual tuning-in relationship" as an "indispensable condition of all possible communication" [22] provides one concrete example of the larger project in which he was engaged: the systematic description of the structures of the life-world. The Gebserian approach I have presented here may also be seen in that light. However, the radical significance of Gebser's notion of "mutations of consciousness" should not be overlooked. Since for Gebser "consciousness" is correlative to "world," and since both terms in the correlation are conceived a) contexturally and b) as structures of possibility rather than as objects granted this or that ontological status, the Gebserian notion of mutation suggests that there may be more than one genuinely operative life-world.

The paradigmatic force of a life-world unrecognized as such by those who dwell in it—those who simply maneuver in it as the reality tacitly assumed in everyday affairs—is such that alternatives may be literally inconceivable. Thus seemingly incomprehensible blocks to communication may arise when two life-worlds, each a genuine and complete "reality" in its own right, clash. On the other hand, the very recognition of the notion of a "life-world" may begin the process of making one's fundamental tacit assumptions diaphanous. Once a pattern of typifications is revealed, it may be taken as one possibility among others; liberated from the rigidity of a single style of being-in-the-world, we may engage in a "mutual tuning-in relationship" with an Other whose usual way of "singing the world" (Merleau-Ponty) finds its usual expression in a music vastly different from our own. Furthermore, we can begin to discern several contextures co-present in a given experience, diaphonously sounding through one another like voices in a piece of contrapuntal music.

Schutz himself allows for the possibility of a "contrapuntal" communicative relationship founded on the possibility of living

22. Schutz, p. 161.

together simultaneously in "several dimensions of time."[23] Within the language of the present paper, this may be stated as follows: the mutual tuning-in relationship may be seen as the establishment or assumption of a tacit contract originating in the possibility of living together simultaneously in one or more "schemes of reference" involving specific qualitative articulations of world-dimensions such as time, space, movement, and corporeality—which shape the background contexture for interpersonal communication in the traditional sense, as well as for other aspects of social interaction (including the very texture of the self-world relationship).

23. Schutz, p. 175; cf. p. 162.

Communicability

Hugh J. Silverman

The creation of a common life-world is the ground for communication. By showing that other persons are not only a
possibility, but a necessary possibility, we approach an
understanding of what it means to be in-the-world. Yet there
is more to this interpersonal life-world than our co-
existence. We also have the possibility of interacting and
communicating with each other. The possibility of communication is both one among many human meanings (more specifically, I am a person who can communicate with other people)
and the active texture of a person's experiential meanings.
In **Reason and Existenz,** [1] Karl Jaspers describes this
possibility of communication as "communicability."

Communicability is more than just the plurality of persons
which I can experience as present in my phenomenal field.
It is the potential for encounter, understanding, and appreciation. I shall describe this potential as the possibility
of shared meanings. Sharing can be of three different
varieties: (1) physical, (2) conceptual, and (3) experiential.

(1) Sharing in the physical sense usually implies a division:
I'll give you some and keep the rest for myself. Here both
persons in question do not take the same material portion.
Sharing a cake means that one person eats part of it and
the other eats what remains. We physically share the world
in that we cannot all occupy the same territory. As Hegel
pointed out in the chapter on "sense-certainty," in the

INTERPERSONAL COMMUNICATION: Essays in Phenomenology and Hermeneutics,
ed., Joseph J. Pilotta, Copyright 1982, The Center for Advanced Research in
Phenomenology, Inc. and co-published by arrangement with The University Press
of America, Inc.

1. See Karl Jaspers, VERNUNFT UND EXISTENZ (Bremen: Johs. Storm, 1949).
English translation by William Earle as REASON AND EXISTENZ (Noonday, 1955).

Phenomenology of Mind, [2] what is Here is not Above or Below, Before or Behind. When considered in terms of the human body, it becomes clear that I am Here and not There. And what is crucial to sharing, when I am Here, you cannot also be Here. You must be There or Elsewhere. At most, you can be in close proximity to Here. In terms of territory, no two people can be in the exact same place at the same time. We share our interpersonal world by occupying different places in it, but nevertheless by participating in it together. To communicate, we must be in different locations, as defined by our bodies. We **physically** share our world -- this is our material being with others, -- we do not physically share our meanings. Meanings, which are not material, cannot be shared physically.

(2) In the conceptual sense, many persons have the same human meanings **in common,** even though they may never actually encounter one another. People often share meanings conceptually "without knowing it." These meanings are not diminished or divided but rather multiplied by the sharing. By this form of sharing, people have a basis for communication. As Spinoza noted, "passion divides, reason unites."[3] In conceptual sharing, human meanings are united through reason. Passion, for Spinoza, causes material division (as in physical sharing). Through reason, -- through common attitudes, common ideas, and common conceptions -- ideas are conceptually shared. In believing that peace is to be preferred over war, two or more people can hold the same view at the same time. I would not have had to hear of Ghandhi to share this notion in common with him.

(3) In experiential sharing, two distinct "parts" or material portions do not arise as in physical sharing. The process remains whole. As in conceptual sharing, that which one shares experientially is kept in common by both (or all) persons involved in the process. Unlike conceptual sharing, however, there is an addition of meaning. Learning has occurred. Hence, it is necessary that an encounter of some sort take place between the persons who are sharing experientially. When Socrates characteristically states (in this case to Protagoras), "If you can demonstrate more plainly to us that virtue is something that can be taught, please don't hoard your wisdom but explain,"[4] he is making an appeal for experiential sharing. He requests that Protagoras impart

2. G.W.F. Hegel, PHÄNOMENOLOGIE DES GEISTES IN WERKE IN ZWANZIG BÄNDEN, 3 (Suhrkamp, 1970), pp. 82–92. English translation by J.B. Baillie as THE PHENOMENOLOGY OF MIND (Harper and Row, 1931), pp. 149–160.

3. Benedict de Spinoza, THE ETHICS, trans. R.H.M. Elwes (Dover, 1883).

4. Plato, PROTAGORAS, p. 320b–c.

some of his wisdom, that he experientially share it with Socrates and the others. In this way, Socrates and the others might become persons who know whether virtue can be taught. Yet we must not ignore the fact that Socrates himself enters into experiential sharing when he requests that Protagoras explain what he knows. In both cases, there will have been an addition of meaning for all members concerned. This new meaning will have been experientially shared.

Let us now consider some possible forms of communication in terms of these three varieties of sharing. This will provide us with a basis for understanding the importance of communicability as a meaning of human being and as the possibility of producing new meanings.

For a long time, it had been assumed that one's body -- the body through which one lives in the world and encounters other people -- was entirely one's own. A person could not physically share it, except perhaps in the act of love, in which case, there is also experiential sharing of one being with another. The notion of "giving" which is continually emphasized by Erich Fromm in **The Art of Loving,**[5] is particularly characteristic of physical sharing. However, if the act of love is also taken to be an imparting in which both partners share, in which both members gain new meaning through the physical sharing, in which both **give** and neither **takes** but both **gain** through the experience, then experiential sharing will also have occurred.

Through heart, kidney, and other transplants, much of the traditional view that we cannot otherwise physically share ourselves is denied. Of course, rituals in which two men could become blood brothers by a mixing of their bloods was a step in this direction. However, even in such rituals, the blood of one Indian brave was not necessary for the functioning of the other. This was very much a form of experiential sharing, based on the view that such mixing of bloods would unite them more closely, -- a view which they both conceptually shared. On the other hand, blood transfusions (along with various organ transplants -- these being dramatic examples of physical sharing of meanings) are usually necessary for survival. They also indicate that the "embodied subject," as Merleau-Ponty has called it, is ambiguous even on the physical level.[6] One's "circuit of existence" continues after the operation, but it is varied by new meanings, for

5. Erich Fromm, THE ART OF LOVING (Bantam, 1956).

6. For an expanded discussion of this point see my "Merleau-Ponty's Human Ambiguity," THE JOURNAL OF THE BRITISH SOCIETY FOR PHENOMENOLOGY, Vol. 9, no. 1 (January 1979), pp. 23-38.

example, a person living with a different heart. In terms
of this circuit of existence, the person remains a functioning
whole despite the removal of one or more organs and its (or
their) replacement by another. In each of these cases, a vital
element of one person subsequently acts as a vital element
in another. As in all cases of physical sharing, what one
person gains, the other person loses. Cannibalism, however,
is not an example of physical sharing, since the new element
does not have the same function in the cannibal's alimentary
processes as it had in its original human context. The central
point here is that, as much as we expect that our physical
being is reserved for ourselves, we find that it is not entirely separate from that of others. Here too there can be
communication: the communication of functioning organs. In
physico-vital examples, the sharing of meanings is restricted
to an exchange. The kidney or blood that I give is no longer
an integral part of my vital functioning. In heart transplants,
the donor is even expected to die.

Physical sharing in medicine has its analogue in conceptual
matters. We assume that our thoughts are private. We assume
that they cannot be shared. But our very thoughts organize
themselves within a conceptual scheme. They are significantly
influenced, as Whorf pointed out, [7] by the very language
we use. They are influenced by the values of those around
us. They are influenced by the technology that permeates
our modern existence. These thoughts may be conceptually
shared in that others hold them too. Yet, my specific employment of them, my thinking, my choosing, my believing, **qua**
processes, are my own. My individual processes are my individuality, my doing what I do establishes what I cannot share.
I can never conceptually share my **individuality of** thinking,
knowing, acting, etc.

I can share the fact that I think, since we all can think;
I can share some of my thoughts because of common conceptual
schemata; I can share some of my thoughts through direct
communication; but I cannot share **all** the individual thoughts
that I think; nor can I share **my specific acts** of thinking.
I can physically share my body with another in that I can
give of myself to him or her. I can create with the other,
but my circuit of existence (that which constitutes my being)
cannot be shared **qua** my own existence. I live my own
existence; it is my individuality. What I share conceptually
are my own meanings, but not my particular singular acts
of experience.

---

7. Benjamin Lee Whorf, LANGUAGE, THOUGHT, AND REALITY (MIT Press, 1956).

There are a number of ways in which my meanings can be
shared conceptually and through which my being-in-the-world
is elucidated. Language is perhaps the most apparent way
in which communicability is established. We all learn a language from early childhood. The language then becomes one
of the principal ways in which we express, experience, and
conceive of the world. Since many people learn the same
language which others learn, often without knowing one
another, they sometimes understand the world in a similar
fashion. They conceptually share their language. In this
respect, language is a series of conventions which they accept
when they learn a particular language.

Language is also active, just as we are always active.[8]
It changes through use and clarification. Through language,
I experientially share linguistic and human meanings with
other people, just as I experience and create my human
meanings through my body. As my body is always a central
and active part of my being-in-the-world, similarly language,
as a **modus communicationis**, is an actualizing of my being-
in-the-world. Language is a vehicle for encounter, understanding, and appreciation. It brings us into contact with
one another, and it enhances that association. Language is
the manner in which we are more than just the condition for
one another. Language is the phenomenon which indicates
that our world is not just an interpersonal framework but
also a context in which we can communicate with one another.
More than just being together in-the-world, we can share
and interact in it through language.

The common view of meanings is that they are primarily
linguistic. In fact, however, meanings have a much wider
application -- there can also be human meanings. Language
is only one respect in which meanings appear. Words have
meaning only because someone speaks, reads, hears, or writes
them. I am and have many meanings; some of which I can
express or communicate through words. For example, when I
am a person who is saying "hello," or simply a person who
is speaking, that can be considered as one of my human
meanings. But expressing through words would be a fruitless
and, in fact, impossible task if I had only myself to speak
to, if there were not also the possibility of conceptually and
experientially sharing what I express with others. Assuming
that the world is an interpersonal one, in which I can
express meanings through words to other persons, the
possibility of communicating is available to me. When I express
meanings through words, the meanings do not precede the

---

8. See my article "Artistic Creation and Human Action," MOSAIC: Literature
and Ideas, Vol. 8, no. 1 (Fall 1974), pp. 157-164.

words. Meanings are expressed **through** words, and, in experiential sharing, the words may be actualized at the same time as the meanings. The words I speak or write are an integral part of who I am. In that respect, I experientially share the meanings of these words with other people.

I can also share linguistic meanings **conceptually** because they occur in the context of a language which we speak in common, but also because our frames of reference coincide sufficiently for us to understand one another. I do not have to meet someone to conceptually share meanings with him. However, to experientially share meanings, encounter through some medium is necessary. This encounter may be in terms of direct presence, writing, a painting, or even an electronic medium such as film, television, or radio. Experiential sharing occurs when encounter and understanding arise. Agreement is not a necessary condition for experiential sharing, since hostility, friendship, disapproval, approval, etc. may characterize the experiential sharing of meanings. However, encounter is necessary, and the encounter often takes the form of linguistic exchange.

Linguistic meanings have symbolic value, as we learn from Cassirer.[9] If words were not symbols, we would only react to them in some behaviorally constant fashion. In the case of symbols, we are not faced with an essentially stimulus-response situation (as behaviorists have suggested), rather we can have many possible undetermined meanings and responses that might be related to the specific word in question. In the experiential sharing of symbols, our emphasis must be placed on the meanings that are understood. But symbols are inseparable from the meanings which experientially arise through them. Existential ambiguity is a condition of meanings in the human situation.[10] I am ambiguous due to the plurivocity of my meanings (but necessarily also in terms of my experience and creation of them). A symbol calls attention to some of these human meanings. We encounter another person and his meanings to some extent through symbols. Hence, if I am a person who is talking with a friend, I make gestures, I look at him, I tell him that I do not agree with him. These are all meanings that constitute my being, but they are also meanings which I experientially share with him, -- we communicate. Our language of words and/or gestures is **communicable** because we conceptually share

9. See Ernst Cassirer, THE PHILOSOPHY OF SYMBOLIC FORMS, 3 vols., trans. Ralph Manheim (Yale University Press, 1957).

10. A more fully developed presentation of existential ambiguity can be found in my "Dasein and Existential Ambiguity" in HEIDEGGER'S EXISTENTIAL ANALYTIC, ed. Frederick A. Elliston (Mouton, 1978), pp. 97-108.

meanings. However, through experiential sharing, this language is actually **communicated.**

In de Saussure's terms, [11] we conceptually share our **langue** (language), while we experientially share our **parole** (speech). Meaning is communicated particularly in **parole.** De Saussure indicates quite precisely the status of meaning in terms of that which signifies (**le signifiant**), for example, the word "tree," and in terms of that which is signified (**le signifié**), for example, the concept tree. In the context of speech, this relation is communicated as meaning (**signification**). In language (**langue**), the relation is conceptually shared as a sign. In experiential sharing, in which there is an addition of human meaning through **signification**, some form of speech (**parole**) is necessary.

De Saussure was principally concerned with a linguistic context. When experiential sharing is considered socially, we find that communication can occur on a direct interpersonal level or, indirectly, in terms of mass communication. It is important to indicate at the outset that neither form of communication is a transfer of meaning. Melvin DeFleur is clear on this point: "The problem of communication is not actually a 'transfer' of meaning. In the communicative act, there is no essence, spirit, or invisible 'something' that leaves the central nervous system of one person and travels to that of another. Such a concept is unnecessary and muddies the water of legitimate inquiry into the nature of human communication with questions about 'thought transference,' 'clairvoyance,' 'mind reading,' and other such inanities."[12] DeFleur, himself, however, sees this experiential sharing as an "**isomorphism** between the internal responses (meaning) to a given set of symbols on the part of both sender and receiver."[13] This isomorphism of response leaves the symbol in a nebulous and, more specifically, non-human status. It is as if we were machines which confer the same form onto whatever material that might be fed into us. The only element that accounts for communication is the similar form of the response in both sender and receiver. This view does not account for the fact that I express my meanings through the language of symbols or words and because of the very words that I use, words that will be or can be understood and

11. Ferdinand de Saussure, COURS DE LINGUISTIQUE GÉNÉRALE (Payot, 1915). See particularly, pp. 97-103 and pp. 158-162. English translation by Wade Baskin as COURSE IN GENERAL LINGUISTICS (McGraw-Hill, 1959), pp. 61-70, and pp. 114-117.

12. Melvin L. DeFleur, THEORIES OF MASS COMMUNICATION (McKay, 1966), p. 91.

13. DeFleur, p. 91.

appreciated, I experientially share these meanings with others. In so doing, I account for the possibility of others answering back. This type of non-physical sharing goes beyond mere **cor-responding** (as Ortega y Gasset has called it)[14] or even isomorphism of response. Isomorphism implies that meanings which I express are always understood in the same way in which they were expressed. Yet we know well that often our words are not understood by others in the same way that they were formulated, — we are often misunderstood. I may respond to what is said by another person without complete isomorphism. Understanding may even occur on the basis of non-identical significations (to return to de Saussure's term). For example, I could say 'cat' and think not only of a four-legged furry animal that purrs, but also more specifically of a Siamese cat, since I have two at home. You, however, may have understood the word in a similar fasion, but may be thinking of your Persian cat. Thus, I express a meaning through the use of a word; you respond to it as I do; but also I offer the word through **parole** as a meaningful expression. You have the possibility of understanding it in that I have experientially shared it with you: it is yours as well as mine. But the manner in which it is yours as well as mine is not always in an identical form, — even though this isomorphism may characterize an ideal condition.

In a full experiential sharing of meanings, the ground exists not only for me to understand you, but also for me to be understood by you. This is not just a mutuality of understanding, an isomorphism of response, but rather an explicit hope that the other person has fully considered what I have said. Or even that he has understood me in a way that I might not have understood myself previously. This is precisely the enhancement of meaning that is essential to experiential sharing. George Orwell, in an essay on Henry Miller, described this situation as "the peculiar relief that comes not so much from understanding as from **being understood.** 'He knows all about me,' you feel; 'he wrote this specially for me!'"[15]

George Herbert Mead, in **Mind, Self, and Society,** attempted to give a theoretical foundation for this sense of considering the other in one's own communicative act. He indicates how we do more than just respond isomorphically when we share meanings experientially. He accounts for our understanding and being understood, for meanings that are both mine and his (or yours), in terms of his notion of the "significant

14. See José Ortega y Gasset, MAN AND PEOPLE, trans. Willard R. Trask (Norton, 1957), ch. 4: "The 'Other Man' Appears," pp. 72-93.

15. George Orwell, "Inside the Whale" in COLLECTED ESSAYS (Anchor, 1957), p. 218.

symbol:"

> When, in any given social act or situation, one individual
> indicates by a gesture to another individual what this other
> individual is to do, the first individual is conscious of the
> meaning of his own gesture -- or the meaning of his gesture
> appears in his own experience -- insofar as he takes the
> attitude of the second individual toward the gesture and
> tends to respond to it implicitly in the same way that the
> second individual responds to it explicitly. Gestures become
> significant symbols when they implicitly arouse in an in-
> dividual making them the same responses which they explicitly
> arouse, or are supposed to arouse, in other individuals,
> the individuals to whom they are addressed.[16]

For Mead, the first individual's gesture, whether it be verbal,
vocal, or otherwise, does not simply call forth a response
which is duplicated in the second individual, as DeFleur would
have it. Rather the first individual takes the meaning of
his own response to his own gesture as a symbol and, at
the same time, takes the response of the other as a symbol.
He offers his own gesture largely in response to the response
of the other. Thus his own symbolized response is really a
reaction to the manner in which he expects that the other
will respond to his gesture. By taking the attitude of the
other into account and implicitly responding to a symbol in
the same way that the other responds to it explicitly, he
performs an act of consideration, an act of communication.
The gesture, then, becomes a significant symbol when it gives
rise to the same response implicitly in me that it does explicitly in you. This relationship is a kind of isomorphism,
but it is not merely that. Mead sees experiential sharing
as an active respect for and assessment of the other's response
in comparison with one's own response to the gesture to be
communicated. What makes it a significant symbol is the
fact that the response of the other has been accounted for
in the formulation of a gesture, such that it will have significance for the other as well. Without this consideration, there
would not really be any communication. There would only
be individual and separate responses, responses which could
themselves indicate that meaning had hardly been shared
at all. At least Mead's view establishes the real possibility
of understanding through communication.

Communicability is this possibility of expression and understanding, the possibility of experientially sharing meaning,
the possibility of both addresser and addressee gaining the
same meaning through interaction.[17] Charles H. Cooley called

16. George Herbert Mead, ON SOCIAL PSYCHOLOGY, ed. Anselm Strauss
(Phoeniz, 1956), pp. 158-9.

17. The notion of "communicability," as presented here, has distinct parallels
with Jürgen Habermas' concept of "communicative competence." See also J.
Habermas, "Towards a Theory of Communicative Competence," INQUIRY, no. 13,
pp. 205-18, 360-75.

this communicability an "impulse to communicate (which) is not so much a result of thought as it is an inseparable part of it."[18] We might claim further that being and the possibility of communicating are inseparable. One cannot be without being in-the-world and one cannot be in-the-world without the possibility of communication. Cooley elaborates upon the impulse to communicate by citing Montaigne's essay on vanity as an expression of this impulse: "There is no pleasure to me without communication; there is not so much as a sprightly thought comes into my mind that it does not grieve me to have produced it alone, and that I have no one to tell it to." But we know well that Montaigne would have made no such observation had he not always been aware that he was communicating in some way, that part of his existence was communicability. Therefore the absence of communication, solitariness, is very real to him. What Jaspers terms "loneliness," has, for him, three characteristics: "First, loneliness is the irremovable pole without which there is no communication. Second, loneliness, as the possibility of an empty I, is a conception of intrinsic nonbeing at the brink of the abyss from which my historic decision to communicate brings me back to reality. Third, loneliness is my present lack of communicative ties to others, and the uncertainty whether this can be helped."[19] Just as life cannot be without death, so too, communication cannot be without loneliness. Loneliness is the meaning of feeling alone. It is the closest one can come to not being at all, and yet it is the very condition that forces us into communication. It makes us aware that we lack communication. This is why, in the tradition of Schopenhauer's "will to live" and Nietzsche's "will to power," Jaspers speaks of a "will to communicate." The "will to communicate" is also a life force, a necessity for existence. The absence of it is loneliness, the total negation of it is death or nonbeing.

Communicability, as suggested by the "will to communicate," is a positive element. It is necessary to the ambiguity of the human condition whose many meanings we continue to create through communication and action. It expands our meanings in that it spreads them out into our world. In this way, we are more than the meanings which would constitute a hypothetical solipsistic self. Thoreau's prose is impeccable in elucidating this point:

18. Charles H. Cooley, HUMAN NATURE AND THE SOCIAL ORDER (Schocken, 1902), p. 92.

19. Jaspers, PHILOSOPHIE (Springer, 1948). English translation by E.B. Ashton as PHILOSOPHY 2 (University of Chicago Press, 1970).

I would fain communicate the wealth of my life to men, would really give them what is most precious in my gift, I would secrete pearls with the shell-fish and lay up honey with the bees for them, I will sift the sunbeams for the public good. I know no riches I would keep back. I have no private good unless it be my peculiar ability to serve the public. This is the only individual property. Each one may thus be innocently rich. I enclose and foster the pearl till it is grown. I wish to communicate those parts of my life which I would gladly live again.[20]

This will to reveal all is the possibility of bringing people closer together, of uniting individual meanings with those of others, of sharing meanings. This "need to impart" is what both Cooley and Max Scheler have called "sympathy." Sympathy is more than Husserl's "empathy," it is a concrete bringing together, rather than a theoretical escape from the ego-centric predicament. "The growth of personal ideas through intercourse implies a growing power of sympathy, of entering into and sharing the minds of other persons. To converse with another, through words, looks, or other symbols, means to have more or less understanding or communion with him, to get on common ground and partake of his ideas and sentiments."[21] Sympathy is the "sharing of any mental state that can be communicated."[22] This sharing is clearly experiential.

Sympathy **qua** sharing of meanings is the interchange of meanings between persons. An intimate dialectic underlies sympathy. Through sympathy there can be negotiation and dialogue. Here meanings are offered only in the sense that they occur in a situation. Experiential sharing of meanings is not only what I do (as in dialogue and in negotiation), but also what arises from the possibilities of my situation, of my being in a world with other persons. As Merleau-Ponty puts it, "communication between consciousnesses is not based on the common meaning of their respective experiences, for it is equally the basis of that meaning."[23] Communicability establishes the possibility for sharing common meanings through sympathy. In this sense, Merleau-Ponty's description of communication demonstrates that a humanly meaningful situation brings about common meanings through sympathetic communication. Thus sympathy is both a giving and a gaining of the

20. Henry David Thoreau, WALDEN as quoted in Cooley, pp. 93-4.

21. See Max Scheler, WESEN UND FORMEN DER SYMPATHIE (F. Cohn, 1923). English translation by Peter Heath as THE NATURE OF SYMPATHY (Yale University Press, 1954).

22. Cooley, p. 136.

23. Maurice Merleau-Ponty, PHÉNOMÉNOLOGIE DE LA PERCEPTION (Gallimard, 1945). English translation by Colin Smith as PHENOMENOLOGY OF PERCEPTION (Routledge and Kegan Paul, 1962), p. 185.

total human significance of the other.

The focus of this discussion of communicability has dealt with communication in terms of verbal language. There are many other "languages" or modes of expression that can be the ground for and manifestation of experientially sharing meanings. Perhaps the most closely related to verbal communication is verbal non-communication. Often when we really don't want to answer a question or feel that the situation is inappropriate to reveal certain reflections, we engage in non-communication. José Luis Aranguren in his study of human communication offers some examples: "There are evidently messages that are not intended to be understood, or rather that have no real content. A politician who is anxious to get out of a tight corner and fills his speeches with common-places and vague expressions that amount to nothing; a diplomat who talks merely to gain time until he receives exact instructions; a pseudo-thinker who conceals reality beneath 'ideas' that are totally alien to it -- these are a few examples of the many instances of such use of language."[24] Similarly Ionesco in **La Cantatrice chauve (The Bald Soprano)** [25] has shown, through exaggeration, how a married couple can live and talk together for years and yet be quite oblivious to one another. In each of these instances, communicability has not been denied. On the contrary, the very experience which arises from such a situation of non-communication magnifies the meanings that are shared. Here only the symbols are made common. But the possibility of sympathy as it arises from the situation continues to be real.

Silence is a similar form of non-linguistic communication. When we do not speak at all, we force communicability to its limits. The lack of expression is a concrete way of uncovering the nature of expression. The felt absence is evidence of our being-in-the-world. It is one of the clearest ways of formulating, in our interpersonal world, that we are there. Our refusal to share is an affirmation of our possibility to share. In Ingmar Bergman's film **Persona** (1966), an actress, who never speaks, befriends, infuriates, and frustrates her nurse, who talks all the time. Although one might think that this situation would inhibit experiential sharing, on the contrary, each woman's "expression" counter-balances and unites her with the other. Bergman seems to use the two women as a personification of communicability itself. By never appealing to a flashback technique, he emphasizes the

---

24. José Luis Aranguren, HUMAN COMMUNICATION, trans. F. Partridge (McGraw-Hill, 1967), p. 137.

25. Eugene Ionesco, LA CONTATRICE CHAUVE IN THÉÂTRE I (Gallimard, 1954).

face-to-face value of the communication that arises. As Pascal said: "Silence is the greatest persecution," [26] it torments us and yet shows us that we cannot escape the viability of communicating with one another. In this way, we know that communication is the ground of meaning. For Kierkegaard, [27] the only true communication, as opposed to that of objective thinking or ordinary communication, is the secrecy of indirect communication. Silence is the expression of subjectivity which can surpass the ethical. Silence, as Kierkegaard shows by the pseudonym for his authorship of **Fear and Trembling:** Johannes de Silentio, is the way towards inward communication, which (he claims) is truth. The paradox of communicability, for Kierkegaard, lies in the affirmation of the ethical and the transcendence of it. Thus as Jaspers remarks "The ultimate in thinking as in communication is silence."[28] "There is a time to keep silent and this silence lies in the continuity of communicative becoming."[29]

Non-verbal communication opens up other dimensions of communicability. Gesture is perhaps the most closely related to spoken language in that, except in writing, it always goes with speech. The nod of a head, the clapping of hands, the wave are all modes of expression. Their possibility within a given culture or group of people provides a further manifestation and assurance of being-in-the-world with others. "The communication or comprehension of gestures," says Merleau-Ponty, "comes about through the reciprocity of my intentions and the gestures of others, of my gestures and intentions discernible (**lisibles**) in the conduct of other people. It is as if the other person's intention inhabited my body and mine his."[30] This reciprocity establishes communicability. The sharing of gestures and intentions is the experiential sharing of meanings.

Gestures are always in terms of the body. Kinesics, as described by Fast in **Body Language,** [31] studies any non-reflexive or reflexive movement of part, or all, of the body when used by a person to communicate. Bodily expression

26. Blaise Pascal, PENSÉES, bilingual edition, trans. H.F. Stewart (Modern Library, n.d.), pp. 410-411.

27. "Ordinary communication, like objective thinking in general, has no secrets; only a doubly reflected subjective thinking has them. That is to say, the entire essential content of subjective thought is essentially secret, because it cannot be directly communicated. This is the meaning of the secrecy." Søren Kierkegaard, CONCLUDING UNSCIENTIFIC POSTSCRIPT, trans. David F. Swenson and Walter Lowrie (Princeton University Press, 1941), p. 73.

28. Jaspers, REASON AND EXISTENZ, p. 106.

29. Jaspers, PHILOSOPHY 2, p. 68.

30. Merleau-Ponty, p. 215; trans. p. 185.

31. J. Fast, BODY LANGUAGE (Evans, 1970).

is exemplified by a person's tendency to hold his or her arms open to indicate receptivity, or a person's tendency to keep his or her arms and legs close to the body as a suggestion of reserve and doubt. A correlate of body language is what Edward Hall has called proxemics, [32] or the study of personal space. The intimate distance of lovers would not normally be used at a cocktail party by two people who were not at all acquainted. In an American subway car, people tend to avoid actual contact with one another as much as possible, while in a French **Métro**, people are not at all upset by being close to and even touching their neighboring rider. One can distinguish a whole series of distances which people in different cultures observe, including intimate, personal, social, and public distances. These distances are determined by the various situations and circumstances prescribed by or within a given culture. This indicates that communicability has its ground in spatial as well as linguistic and bodily terms. Just as languages are culturally defined (some people speak English, others speak Japanese), various spatial customs operate within different cultures. There are, then, greater barriers when I seek to share my meanings experientially with others or even for the possibility of that sharing to occur when I am in another country, particularly one where I do not speak that language or know the customs. In these cases I also conceptually share less than I would at home.

Edward Hall relates an example of the lack of communication due to the absence of conceptual sharing in his book **The Silent Language.** An American agriculturalist, who was sent to a Latin American country as an attaché of the United States Embassy, went to see a local governmental minister. After having arrived several minutes early (the American respect pattern), he waited outside the minister's office for forty-five minutes. Not realizing that a delay of up to an hour was a tolerable custom there, the American became irate and let the minister's secretary know that he was "damn sick and tired" of this sort of treatment. The minister (interpreting the American as impertinent) replied: "Let him cool his heels." In this instance, both men, through ignorance of the other's customs, experientially shared a lack of understanding. For those who conceptually share customs, the possibility of employing time, as well as space, can be a necessary condition of communicability.

Other forms of communication might include eating habits, such as those which Lévi-Strauss relates in **The Raw and**

---

32. See Edward Hall, THE SILENT LANGUAGE (Anchor, 1959). Hall has also investigated other aspects of non-verbal communication in THE HIDDEN DIMENSION (Anchor, 1969).

Cooked, [33] and dress fashions, which Roland Barthes carefully outlines in **Système de la mode**.[34] As in all of our examples of communication, there must be conceptual sharing for actual experiential sharing to arise. Customs of preparing foods, setting the table, greeting one another, dressing, etc. must all be understood in common before meaning can be enhanced within any of these realms. In **Reason and Existenz,** Jaspers makes the claim that reason and rationality are the very ground and possibility of communication. But reason is not simply shared conceptually, for it is through reason that we open ourselves to one another. Reason is the medium in which we establish our mutualilty, in much the same way that language, the body, gestures, space, and time are conditions for communication. Through reason, we find and experience meaning in-the-world. Through reason, human meanings are rendered manifest. The Greeks called reason **logos** -- the very structure or scheme of being itself. Reason or **logos** allows us to display the interpersonal features of our existence. Without reason we could not experientially share meanings. The actual working out of thought or knowledge through reason and reasoning is our experiential sharing of meanings, which is the essence of communication. The possibility of communication as itself a human meaning permeates all of our personal meanings. This communicability is fundamental to our being-in-the-world.

The three types of sharing (physical, conceptual, and experiential) are each characterized by that which is shared: things, ideas, and human meanings respectively. When sharing things, we already understand conceptually what we share physically. We understand and know things in particular ways because of the language, conceptual schemes, etc. that are available to us. Without knowledge of something shared (except through the most accidental conditions), apportionment could not occur materially. A commonality of shared ideas is necessary for the experiential sharing of things, ideas, and human meanings. Experiential sharing is already present in the material entity that is apportioned (given and taken), -- for the division of things arises through human activity and the creation of meanings. Experiential sharing, therefore, noetically accounts for the noemata (things, ideas, or human meanings) which are appropriated and understood in common.

33. Claude Lévi-Strauss, LE CRU ET LE CUIT (Paris: Plon, 1964). English translation by John and Doreen Weightman as THE RAW AND THE COOKED: Introduction to a Science of Mythology, vol. I (Harper and Row, 1969).

34. Roland Barthes, SYSTÈME DE LA MODE (Seuil, 1967).

The purpose of this essay has been to account for the possibility of communication. How we do or do not succeed at particular acts of communication is not my concern here. Yet the realization of experiential sharing does indeed fulfill these conditions of communicability. With the sharing of things and ideas, the minimal ground of communication has been established. Common participation in the creation and overdetermination of human meanings grounds the type of rationality (**logos**) which a life-world encompasses, including individuals in isolation seeking to communicate, the performance of silence, dialogical and plurilogical interlocution, group decisions, passionate attachment, dionysian festivals, and congressional enactments of law. Such common participation is the basis for communicability.[35]

35. A version of this text was initially presented at the Conference on Cross-Cultural Phenomenology, held at the Ontario Institute for Studies in Education, Toronto (Canada), June 27-29, 1977. These concluding remarks respond to comments by members present at the session, especially Friedrich Sixel, Joseph Pilotta (who organized the conference), Elizabeth Behnke, and Algis Mickunas. I am grateful for their reflections.

The Philosophical Problem
of the Objective
Historical Sciences

Tim L. Widman

Introduction

The significance of Gadamer's hermeneutical philosophy for
the human sciences can be summarized in two propositions.
First, historical understanding fundamentally misrepresents
its own nature and distorts its relation with its objects when
it relegates its historicality to the status of sheer prejudice
and for this reason endeavors to close itself off to history
in order to recoup history absolutely through methodical
reappropriation.[1] Second, in acknowledging its inherent
positionality (factical finitude) historical understanding
recognizes that the reason which guides it is always conditional historical reason inseparable from the situation in
which it operates. As the consequence, the primary datum
of hermeneutical self-understanding, the self-understanding
of the human historical sciences, is the continuity of history
with the present of historical reflection and, therefore, the
requirement that historical understanding comprehend itself
as belonging within a process of historical mediation.

For Gadamer, understanding is first of all communication.
The task of historical hermeneutics has been to overcome the
alienation of meaning time has created for the sake of maintaining the process of communication with the past, which
forms the tradition. Moreover, these two propositions admit
reformulation into alternative communications models. His
assessment of objective historical understanding, methodical

INTERPERSONAL COMMUNICATION: Essays in Phenomenology and Hermeneutics,
ed., Joseph J. Pilotta, Copyright 1982, The Center for Advanced Research in Phenomenology, Inc. and co-published by arrangement with The University Press of
America, Inc.

1. Hans-Georg Gadamer, TRUTH AND METHOD (Seabury Press, 1975), p. 251.
Hereafter cited as TM.

understanding, regards it as the systematic attempt to reflect oneself out of any relation with the Thou, to refuse to be addressed by the other, as the prerequisite for transmuting this other into a source of information about itself. Such objectification establishes an epistemological detachment which replaces the communicative possibility with cognitive domination. The alternative, the dialogue, is fulfilled in the dialectic of question and answer in which a common meaning emerges on the basis of reciprocal determination of reflective horizons (fusion of horizons). This model presupposes a specific kind of openness: not the dissimulating openness of unbiased disinterest or even, as Gadamer is sometimes taken to intend, openness to the "Thou" as such, but rather openness to mediation by what is said in the conversing; a kind of openness which assumes active participation and interest on the part of the speakers in behalf of the truth of what is said. One might venture to suggest that what is required for dialogue is an **integrating element** through which the conversers, that is to say, their persons and the reflective-historical horizons, become transparent in a way that lets the meaningfulness of what is said, rather than the speaking or the speakers, become thematic and decisive.

But this is only to illustrate an insight that pertains to the entirety of the human historical sciences (**Geisteswissenschaften**). This paper will attempt to secure this insight, though to be sure only one aspect of it. The second proposition mentioned above contains Gadamer's reversal of the prejudice against prejudice and expresses the substance of his reflection upon language. It is, however, the first proposition that will occupy us here. This first, primarily critical proposition is important for two reasons. First, far from promoting historicism, much less existential capriciousness, Gadamer's central theme is reason; reason in the metaphysical sense, transcendence. Indeed, the crucial problem for hermeneutical reflection must be the retrieval of historical reflection from the methodological self-consciousness whose effect upon the human studies has been, as will become evident, to render their results either irrational or trivial. Second, only a sustained critique of objectivism can make plain the warrant for a Gadamerian approach in the human studies. Much more than that, only such a critique demonstrates the transcendental necessitation for this reappraisal. For Gadamer's criticisms of the historical consciousness are directed ultimately to the nature of reflection itself. It is for us to consider this critique in its greatest generality, namely, as the problem of reflection in the historical sciences, in order to assert its relevance beyond the restricted concerns of any single historical scientific discipline and thereby approximate its full compass.

Is thinking at all possible in the context of the modern consciousness of history? That this question appears too abstract to be a genuine question or that the answer is in any case a matter of course only confirms the measure of historical reflection's enfeeblement by its preoccupation with method. As reason, a relation of suspended immediacy, thinking is permanently determined as transcendence. Transcendence, in turn, has reality only in the actuality of what transcends. What for thinking is transcendent is truth or, in the language of Classical metaphysics, the truth of what is, namely, being. Thus thinking is the rational relationship: a persisting orientation defined by the transcendence of its object.

It is thought's own fecundity, its almost profligate productivity, that first suggests through the record of its achievements the impossibility of thinking. History indexes the multiple unsystematic variability of thought's progeny, and historically sophisticated deliberation upon them begins by acknowledging in each their intrinsic uniqueness and validity insofar as they all represent objective possibilities of historical human existence. In the seemingly limitless variety of historically specific forms affecting every aspect of human experience, reflection encounters itself strewn across time and comes up against its inherent historical impermanence as a kind of self-imposed negation. This self-estrangement originating in reflection's own historical reality reduces transcendence to an impotent ideal or an irrational credal object and posits history as an indomitable surd forever transforming thought into its opposite.

Philosophical hermeneutics is motivated by the conviction that truth remains the indispensable premise of thinking. For Gadamer, historicism marks the collapse of the direct tradition of philosophical questioning;[2] its renewal can be effected only through the appropriation of the truth of the modern experience of history and the recovery of historical reflection from the impasse of historical objectivism. Thus Gadamer's struggle with historical hermeneutics and the historical method represents the attempt to realize the unfulfilled promise of the historical consciousness. Despite its having produced a positive corrective to the subjective self-consciousness by demonstrating the hidden historical positionality in every case necessarily mediating that consciousness, the historical consciousness continues to conceive itself on the model of subjective consciousness. Accordingly, the historical consciousness confines the relation of reflection to its historicality within the narrowness of an epistemological concept which defines history as a possible object of knowledge and

2. Ibid., p. 339.

historical understanding as the methodically rigorous process of acquiring objective knowledge of history. Consequently, understanding seeks its essence in a freely chosen relation to its objects.

Accomplishing this scientific ideal is conditional upon a reflective universality that is immediate to all historical phenomena by virtue of its formal inclusion of any possible historical viewpoint. Only in this way can the historical consciousness secure direct access to its objects in the specific immediate objective unity of their distinct historical contexts. In other words, only thus does it become possible to articulate historical phenomena as the particular, dynamic, immanent structures that they are in themselves. Historical understanding precludes thereby the vitiation of its results that would ensue from the mediation of its objects by some historically specific commitment—a commitment all the more inimical to reason were it to be unintentional. As the result, the historical consciousness identifies the rational unity of thought with the formal universality of its method, before which the coequal validity of all specific historical expressions does not derive from the objective content of the meanings themselves, because indeed it is precisely the nature of the historical particularity of these expressions that they would mediate one another, but results instead from the collective relativity of historical expressions as such from the standpoint of the absolute consciousness articulated by the universal historical method.

It is indicative of the historical consciousness' unkept promise, what Gadamer calls its self-alienation, [3] that its historical destiny has implicated it in positivist metaphysics (aesthetic historical positivism). The metaphysics of particularity (historicism) and the metaphysics of individuality (Romantic hermeneutics) model historical truth on the static abstract determinateness of anonymous objective relationships. Whether the relation between thought and reality is formulated, as it is by the former, in the generalized particularity designated by the category of historical life-forms or whether it is formulated, as it is for the latter, in the concepts of original authorship and contemporary reader, it is substructed by a fixed, specifiable complex of historically contingent relations defining it in all cases as a specific historical object. On this view, historical understanding must be conceived as a kind of invariant noninterference with its objects that is established and guaranteed by the rational ahistoricality of its method. In understanding itself as a scientific consciousness that distances itself from its objects for the sake of the rational autonomy of epistemological neutrality,

3. Ibid., p. 272.

the historical consciousness effectively disjoins reason from history and nullifies the very historical dimension at work in the consciousness of truth that it itself has unearthed.

In pursuit of the legitimate ideal of interpreting historical phenomena through their own concepts, historical understanding determines its objects in their relation to their historical milieu as a relation of parts to a whole. Accordingly, the analysis of historical meaning proceeds on the basis of its relatedness to selected relevant elements constitutive of the total life-historical situation to which it belongs, including such determinants as social, material, stylistic, linguistic, psychological, and intellectual components. The epistemological principle governing this approach maintains that no meaning is comprehensible immediately in the isolated totality it presents, but only "historically" by way of the complex historical-psychological individuality it expresses and which defines the point of view appropriate to it.[4] Valid understanding occurs only as the harmony of all details with a whole, only when the understanding of meaning merges with the understanding of the structural **whole** forming meaning's historical present.[5] Understanding is actual, that is to say, understanding becomes historical knowledge, only in the perfected convergence of meaning with historical context as an aspect integrated within a reconstructed historical horizon.

The specific differentia of historical-hermeneutical understanding, which distinguishes it in principle from sheer reiteration, is the properly synthetic character of its reproductive procedure. The reconstructive method defines the content of its object by resolving it into the fixed possibilities of the closed circle of expression forming the underlying hidden unity of historical reality. By converting the ostensible transcendence of meaning with respect to ontological reality into the finite totality of relationships composing the horizon of a historical object, understanding makes explicit the immanent historicality of its object. The reproductive achievement of the original horizon of meaning consists therefore of raising the "for itself" of mediate universality to the "in itself" characterizing the immediate unity of an object of knowlege. This reconstructive turning of meaning back upon its original situation forms a synthetic reflective dimension, namely, "historical expression," by employing the necessary historicality of historical phenomena as the single valid interpretative horizon guiding legitimate understanding. In this way, historical meaning can be reproduced as an objectively

4. Ibid., p. 301.

5. "Whole" here can have many constructions. We are using it broadly as subjective-historical individuality.

determinable relation of the past with itself--more accurately, of "some" historicality with itself, because it is precisely the constitutive operation of historical time, historical distance, that is disengaged here.[6] On this basis, any proposition about the world becomes knowledge about a histori- cally specific world; meaning and history are reconciled in the concept of historical datum. The nature of historical- hermeneutical understanding is precisely understanding the past--more generally, the "historically other"--better than it was possible for the past to understand itself; because, to be sure, the past could not become a given totality for itself, much less regard itself as an object for progressive research. Thus the reconstructive appropriation of objects through the universal interpretative horizon of historicality as such constitutes the rational essence of understanding as a process and produces its scientific status.[7]

Gadamer traces the development of this scientific impulse, [8] a development which corresponds to the evolution of historical consciousness, from the Romantic hermeneutics of genius through Dilthey's reformulation of the entire Geisteswissenschaften, wherein, Gadamer maintains, hermeneuti- cal rationalism culminates in the illusion of perfected histori- cal enlightenment, in the ideal of the "total opening of our historical horizon, the abolition of our finiteness in the infinity of knowledge, the omnipresence of the historically knowing spirit."[9] The illusion of a priveleged historical relation is inherent to defining meaning by the objective whole of historical structure. As ontologically determined in its horizon, i.e., forming a historical reality, any meaning can remain self-identical only within its horizon. Consequently, the sole relation possible for understanding with respect to its objects is cumulative knowledge about what they have to say about themselves, what historical situation they bear witness to; understanding is the articulation of the synthetic reflective dimension. As the result, rational transcendence exists only at the horizon of historicality as such. The dialectical illusion generated therein proposes a historical

6. This can be stated as an intersubjective model: one of the partners in the dialogue elects to observe the "other," i.e., to put out of play one's own view- point upon what is said in favor of an anonymous, or what is more often the case, a theoretically constructed vantage point. In this application, the dis- tance that is disengaged is, phrased loosely, psychological. The translation of another's utterance by means of a socio-economic, political, or cultural glossary is a commonplace instance of this, if you will, historicized version of solipsism.

7. Ibid., pp. 322-324.

8. Gadamer's use of the word "scientific" can occasion needless confusion. Science and scientific connote for him a specific position or a specific type of position, TM, pp. XII, 336, 409, et passim.

9. TM, p. 306.

transcendence of history, the absolutization of the interpretative horizon of historicality as such, where history becomes
transparent to itself or, more precisely, to a specific historical present, namely, historical understanding. Correlated
to the methodological ideal of a perfected convergence of
meaning with the whole of historical context is the metaphysical ideal of the perfected convergence of the absolute
historical horizon (the telos of history) with historical understanding. History realizes itself in unconditional self-
knowledge, viz., the science of pure historicality, and
establishes actual transcendence of history in the form of
its enlightened mastery by the historically absolutized and
so autonomous self-consciousness exercised by historical consciousness. The failure of traditional hermeneutics and the
historical attitude generally, according to Gadamer, has been
precisely this artificial limitation of its objects to their significance for the past.[10]

The still implicit estrangement of reason and history consequent
to the hermeneutical postulate identifying the significative-
interpretative horizon with the historical horizon reaches
unmistakeable proportions in the historical understanding's
concept of its own historical position. No less than the
objectifying determination of historical phenomena, historical
understanding presupposes a rigorously objective self-relation.
This self-understanding makes it plain that beyond reflection's
suspicion about historical objects, reflection is fundamentally distrustful about itself. This methodological doubt,
calling to mind the Cartesian legacy of modern thought, evolves
in both applications from the recalcitrance of reflection to
think history immanently.

The hermeneutical canon commanding the careful separation
of the context of the interpreter from the context of historical
authorship fulfills the historicizing intention of the historical
consciousness by simultaneously acknowledging the historical
substruction of the reflecting self-consciousness and repudiating
this characteristic historicality of the interpreting subject
as inadmissable to the hermeneutical relation. The subjective-
historical reflective horizon of historical individuality poses
an unavoidable obstacle and an omnipresent threat to historical
knowledge. The systematic restraint upon understanding
responding to this insight is secured in principle by the concept of contemporary reader. Historical understanding dis-
engages the interpreting "I" from the historical "I" by
replacing the historical standpoint of the interpreter with
the original reader or addressee, who define the horizon
of legitimate possibilities for understanding. In this way,

10. Ibid., p. 303.

historical understanding would accomplish the suspension of every understanding present, including not only the viewpoint peculiar to the interpretative present but most especially the gamut of previous understandings composing the tradition of interpretation, save the uniquely proper historical present of the object. Only when one has in this manner removed oneself from the hermeneutical relation in favor of an anonymous historical standpoint does understanding become possible. On the condition that it is not understanding but a particular historical present that is addressed by historical objects, the interpreter or, more properly, understanding can become contemporary with its objects. Objective determination of historical meaning, of any meaning, depends upon this principle of nonmediate access.[11]

This methodologically sophisticated, if historically naive, transiting of historical presents represents, whether practicable or not, an illegitimate ideal.[12] In principle, this canon is self-evident: in order to understand history reflection must understand itself historically. But as part of historical method, it serves merely to axiomatize reflection's embarrassment over its historical essence and proposes to complete their disjunction through liberating reflection in self-objectification, through emptying reflection of all historical commitment. Reflection becomes immune to the effects of history to the extent of its self-objectification, to the degree it achieves a kind of self-evacuating voidance.[13] Historical understanding's emulation of the scientific concept of cognitive objectivity and the resulting attempt to eliminate subjective distortion of historical processes through methodical representation therefore forces all reflection that would understand itself into the unhappy predicament of having first to compromise its rational significance through recasting it as content specific to one possible historical human relation among all others--each of which appear equally and mutually indifferent under the uniform illumination produced by the horizon of historicality as such.

Objective historical understanding presumes the prejudicial nature of historically immanent reflection. The individuality of the interpreter, more generally, the necessary particularity of any possible historical present, exercises an inevitable invalidating influence with respect to any other present and must be neutralized before legitimate understanding can commence.[14] It is only after understanding that the present

11. Ibid., pp. 270-274.
12. Ibid., p. 358.
13. Ibid., p. 186.
14. Ibid., p. 163.

of interpretation can be readmitted, that anything like application or critique can legitimately take place. History obstructs
understanding, and therefore must be transcended. For hermeneutical self-reflection this means that immanently historical
reflection must become the universal interpretative horizon
of pure historicality and the consciousness of method; reflection
must annul history if it is to achieve objective self-understanding.[15]

Correlated to the objective self-reference of the past is the
painstakingly transparent nonreference of the methodically
purified reflecting present; a present therefore capable of
recreating itself perfectly in any historical present as the
understanding of that present.[16] The systematic precondition
for accomplishing objective knowledge of the past is, then,
precisely objective knowledge of the present, i.e., the objectification of history in total is the condition for the application
of objective methods. Hence, the methodological ideal of the
complete self-mediation of the past through the intermediary
of the progressive articulation of the synthetic reflective
dimension necessitates an ideal perfected self-mediation of
the historical present. Only by accomplishing this is reflection
freed from historical content and understanding from historical
bias. This criterion can be satisfied only if reflection is
realized in completed self-knowledge enabling unconditional
critical distance to itself. Such an unconditional self-mediation
of the reflective present, this pure self-relation, would have
the form of a freely reconstructed present exhibiting its inner
unity as a contingent historical reality. This reconstructed
present must be objectified completely; it must not contain
any unnoted possibilities; all historical potentialities must
be actual.[17] In this light, the future becomes problematical
because any supervening present can not be a historical present. In seeking methodological contemporaneity, cognitive
immediacy, with every historical present, historical understanding requires the nullification of the very historical
ground which forms the sine qua non of historical thinking.
Before any history can be objective, all history must be an
object.[18]

The attempt to comprehend historical phenomena entirely within
the unfolding of their conditions and private intentions and
the pursuit of the methodological apparatus consistent with

15. Hans-Georg Gadamer, "The Universality of the Hermeneutical Problem,"
in PHILOSOPHICAL HERMENEUTICS, trans. and ed. David E. Linge (Univ. of
California Press, 1976), p. 5.

16. TM, p. 192.

17. Ibid., p. 204ff.

18. Ibid., pp. 174-175.

this goal leaves historical understanding's own historical self-understanding with a dilemma. It is confronted with two options, each of which are from a historical perspective equally unpalatable. On the one hand, historical understanding must construe its own processes and conclusions to be altogether ideal recombinations and assessments entirely insular with respect to the historical process and necessarily devoid of historical meaning. In this case its efforts are expended to the benefit of an absolute universalized observer and are completely lost on any historically conditional existence. This situation is particularly ironical for the historical consciousness which, in contradistinction to traditional metaphysics and to speculative idealism, postulates a finite historical human essence and the priority of the empirical historical process. Be that as it may, understanding on this model is the pure actuality of knowledge, whose present is a present **sui generis**, viz., pure presence; a presence which in the context of historical experience must be conceived as presentlessness. This sheer act of knowing envisioned by objective history belongs to the tradition of self-evident immediacy presented by the Cartesian **Cogito sum** and beyond that by the first principle of Aristotelean metaphysics, namely, self-thinking-thought. It is epitomized for the modern consciousness by the transcendental world self-constitution propounded in the universal objective egology of Husserlian transcendental phenomenology. On the other hand, historical understanding must simply identify its understanding present with the historical present and thereby commit itself to the ultimate imposture of supposing that history is completed; in other words, that history gives way to historical self-knowledge and historical action is surpassed in rational praxis, autonomous self-creation. In this case, understanding marks the sublation of history in the concept and reflection passes over into ideology. These alternatives, which doubtlessly are not so much alternatives as different aspects of modern subjectivized anthropocentrism, emerge consequentially from the methodological perspective. They obtain whatever the practical limitations imposed by the finitude of historical information and the programmatic model of progressive research. It belongs to the essence of the ethos of conceptual domination, which Gadamer describes, [19] that historical consciousness formulates itself as a detached observer of the historical spectacle playing itself out before it [20] and conceives understanding in the historical sciences on the model of the natural scientific understanding's experimental reproduction of processes in nature.[21]

19. Ibid., p. 409.

20. R.G. Collingwood, THE IDEA OF HISTORY (Oxford Univ. Press, 1976), pp. 175 and 181.

21. TM, p. 336.

When we turn our attention from the consciousness of method and the universal interpretative horizon of historicality as such to the historical world-view of which it is a part, it becomes possible to gauge the rational-historical alienation concretely in its repercussions for the actual historical life of living subjects. In so doing, we focus upon the immanent historical perspective determined by the experience of absolute historicality, which is historical consciousness in its concrete form, namely, as a model of human comportment with the world.

For what does it mean to be historical in this way? The same approach that systematically isolates and detraditionalizes reason makes existence an object to itself as history and history an objective determinant of our being. Historical understanding fixes the individual existent as a point of contact for communal and historical forces, as a composite of observable historical properties, among which number experience and thought as their subjective reflexes. The historicizing determination of meaning as a function of particular historical structures translates human creativity, provided of course that history is ultimately human, into an overwhelming force enslaving him. If every human relation of whatever order is a positive historical reality binding for itself and bounded by determinable possibilities for expression, then such relations are ultimately opaque with respect to themselves both individually and collectively. The nonsensicality of tradition "has become the general rule for historical consciousness." Even "meaning that is generally accessible through reason is so little believed that the whole of the past, even, ultimately, all the thinking of one's contemporaries is seen only 'historically,'" viz., is deemed comprehensible only "by going back to the past's way of looking at things."[22]

The universal devaluation of truth and the acknowledged incomprehensibility of history are inseparable from the absolutization of the objective historical approach. History as conceived by objective historical understanding is, to reapply a classic metaphor, like the night in which all cows are black. In essence, historical relativism asserts the domination of thought by the given; there exists no viewpoint—no concept, no value, no behavior—that is not already the given and its ramification. Consequently, it is not reflection or even experience that dogmatizes about reality, but rather history is itself necessarily dogmatic, and only derivatively human beings. Accordingly, objective historical understanding, even when it avoids reductionism and excessively genetic

22. Ibid., p. 244.

evaluation and remains self-consciously idiographic and descriptive-comparative, presumes that history is unintelligible to itself and, what is philosophically crucial, in it reflection is gratuitous. In short, the finitude of thought and experience educed by the objective historical particularity of our being imposes a far greater limitation upon the human essence than the natural finitude of species characteristics and biological mortality.

Objectifying history in the manner that nature becomes objectified creates a basic existential contradiction for histori-cal life: in objectifying nature, thought asserts man's priveleged mastery of nature and secures his cultural dominion; by objectifying history, thought rescinds this privileged distinction through making thought historical in the way that nature is natural. As the consequence, human existence risks becoming irretrievably lost to itself. Objective nature's blindly determinate indifference, its lawful regularity, pro-vides structured potential for human self-realization; objective history's blindly determinate indifference, its predictably mutable specificity, parodys human existence with the spectacle of an inane, albeit colorful and highly nuanced, succession of life situations.

Once the methodological perspective suspends the question of truth for the sake of securing historical impartiality, it can not be reintroduced, because the realization of objective history entails precisely the exclusion of historical truth.[23] The truth of history is available only to objective historical understanding, and this understanding can occur only outside of the historical process formulated in a language incompre-hensible to historical beings. Thus objective historical under-standing continues, whether willingly or not, traditional meta-physics and especially Christian theology, which latter devalues history as part of its transposition of life and death. Accordingly, Christian theology's eschatological vision is supplanted by the eschaton of enlightened rational autonomy, specifically the ideological-technical elite managing **homo laborens**, while the biblical mythic epiphany of the religious spirit is superceded by the experimental-discursive epiphany of the scientific spirit.[24] Objective history, to which as historical existence we necessarily belong and to which as cognitive existence we dare not belong, restates in terminology appropriate to the modern experience the persisting "two-world"

---

23. Ibid., pp. 269-270.

24. The secular resymbolization of religious doctrine has its roots in the Renaissance transference of divine qualities to the world. Carl Friedrich von Weizäcker, "Das neue Bild vom Weltall," in DIE NEUE WELTSCHAU (Deutsche Verlags-Anstalt, 1952), pp. 52-53.

doctrine of Classical metaphysics and Christian theology ("Platonism" Nietzsche labelled it) and revises in the disjunction of historical meaning and historical understanding the original ontological "chorismos" of existent and being observed of Plato by Aristotle.[25]

Thus the self-alienation of the historical consciousness effects a kind of schizophrenia in historical experience. The counterpart of the methodological exclusion of "ourselves" from historical knowledge in favor of disinterested methodical understanding is the exclusion of "ourselves" from history as rational, meaningful beings. History becomes an independent, autonomously self-actualizing process. History casts back a mirror image of the scientific objectivity of historical understanding in history's disinterested neutrality toward human existence. History posits its own claim to truth by configuring itself as a register highlighting our temporal futility and demonstrating our imprisoned immersion in the stream of history; **we** become the spectacle. History's truth, then, finally, is that history forbids us truth. In which case, the cognitive purity of unbiased historical understanding finds its correlate in the impartial vacuity of historical existence. By way of an illustration, consider only one almost self-explanatory development in French thought wherein positivism is fulfilled in nihilism. Comptean objective historical science (sociology) provides the background for the Sartrean "la nausée" of objective historical existence. The connection between them, put simply, is that objective method and objective existence both have "nothing" as their contents.

The effect of Gadamer's critical survey has been to expose a significant lapse in the radicality of the historical consciousness. This defect, what we have called its unkept promise and Gadamer its self-alienation, has prevented it from acquiring a genuinely historical dimension and from evolving into what is for Gadamer the hermeneutical consciousness.[26] By stopping short of bringing to bear upon itself the same profound historical insight it so diligently pursues in its objects, the scope of hermeneutical reflection has suffered a severe artificial restriction and the legitimacy of the entire hermeneutical enterprise has been left open to question. The difficulties we have described do not originate in some inscrutable disregard for reason on the part of history but constitute the ultimate issue of the resistance to history exhibited by the historical consciousness itself. The direct result of this resistance, which since it is so deeply rooted

25. METAPHYSICS, bk. I, ch. 9.
26. Ibid., p. 267.

in the metaphysical tradition offers a prime illustration of what Gadamer intends by "effective history," is manifest in the failure to ground historical understanding in the very phenomenon whose primordiality for thinking the historical consciousness has itself made inescapable. Accordingly, Gadamer's contribution to hermeneutical theory consists of immanent self-criticism of the historical consciousness, which, much more than sympathetic with its basic inclination, presupposes the validity of the historical approach and attempts to formulate its real universality. Truely historical thinking must acknowledge the historicality of thinking itself and account for movement not only in the process of history but also in the understanding of history.[27]

The radicalizing completion of the historical consciousness in the hermeneutical consciousness proposes that there can be thought about history only by virtue of thought's being itself historical. This thesis expands the historical determination that historical consciousness extends to its objects to include the thought about those objects. This shared historical essence indicates the full setting of hermeneutical inquiry, to be sure, of social scientific reflection.[28] For recognition of "the fundamental unity formed by the historical object and the thinking about that object" [29] shifts the centre of hermeneutical reflection from a priori objectivity and the formal conditions for objective historical knowledge to the "tension that exists between the identity of a common object and the changing situation in which it must be understood."[30]

There is scarcely a more cogent recommendation of the necessary historicality of reflection than in the dilemma objective historical understanding has created for itself through its exclusion of history. In order to construct itself absolutely as objective experience of history, historical understanding had to presume the closure of reflection (historical meaning) within its historical horizon and so insinuate its eclipse. But in so doing, understanding belied the possibility of its own being. This predicament explains in principle the recourse hermeneutics has historically taken to psychological techniques and concepts. But, to be sure, the vitiation of reflection produced by its purification from all historical content presents only negatively the principle that reflection is historical in its essence. It is possible to rescue historical understanding from the absurdity of the historical consciousness,

27. Ibid., pp. 258 and 269.

28. Ibid., p. 232.

29. Ibid., p. 267.

30. Ibid., p. 276.

while simultaneously salvaging the legitimate function of historical consciousness, only through providing the reflective dimension altogether lacking in previous hermeneutical theory. The absence of this dimension accounts for the apparent contradiction in historical understanding between historical consciousness and reflection. The impossibility of reflection within the historical consciousness owes to the fact that historical consciousness and the objective historical understanding founded upon it constitute, as Gadamer repeatedly observes, a naive consciousness; one which is thus fundamentally not yet reflection but only its impetus and provocation. The projection of historical horizons and the determination of the historical particularity of meaning is not where reflection ceases, but where it is first set into motion: it is at this juncture that the task of understanding commences.[31] To say this, however, is to say that historical understanding has neither understood itself when it understands itself as the absolute consciousness of method nor understood its objects when it understands them only historically. It is for this reason that Gadamer directs his attention to the clarification of the self-understanding of historical understanding and portrays the efforts of philosophical hermeneutics as the analysis of the conditions under which understanding takes place. Despite the long and certainly most articulate tradition of hermeneutical self-reflection, the nature of understanding remains undetermined. At the same time, the orientation of historical-hermeneutical reflection is clear: "the task of hermeneutics, seen philosophically, consists in asking what kind of understanding, what kind of science is itself changed by historical change."[32]

31. Ibid., p. 273.
32. Ibid., p. 276.

The Significance of the Phenomenology of Written Discourse for Hermeneutics

Thomas M. Seebohm

Introduction

The thesis of this paper is that the struggle about validation and objectivity in text hermeneutics, which will be outlined in Section 1, can be brought to an end with the aid of a precise phenomenological analysis of the communication patterns which are characteristic for written discourse. Section 2 has the preparatory function of determining the methodological root problem of the struggle in hermeneutics. Section 3 deals with the difference between the communication patterns in oral and written discourse and some specific characteristics of the latter, which are of interest for methodological reasons. Section 4 applies the results of Section 3 to the methodological root problem, identified in Section 2. It will be shown that the claim for objectivity and validity in text hermeneutics is a justifiable claim and that all arguments against it are either based on incomplete descriptions or blur the difference between oral and written discourse in general.

The Context of the Problem

A general answer to the question "What is hermeneutics?" is difficult. In one group of books and articles "hermeneutics" is understood as **one** part of the philological method. The other part is philological and historical critique. In another group "hermeneutics" is considered to be a general theory of understanding and as such the object of philosophical investigations in a variety of philosophical methods: phenomenology, dialectic, transcendental reflections in Kant's style, and the genuine type of **philosophical hermeneutics**

INTERPERSONAL COMMUNICATION: Essays in Phenomenology and Hermeneutics, ed., Joseph J. Pilotta, Copyright 1982, the Center for Advanced Research in Phenomenology, Inc. and co-published by arrangement with The University Press of America, Inc.

which has been developed by Heidegger and his school.[1] Seen from the viewpoint of the older, **methodical philological hermeneutics** this new treatment of hermeneutics in the second half of the twentieth century is confusing—even embarrassing—for the following three reasons:

1. The fact that hermeneutics and critique are inseparable aspects of the philological-historical method is neglected.

2. The second canon of hermeneutics, the canon of the whole and the parts, leading into the famous "hermeneutical circle," is considered to be the more essential one.[2] The first canon, which demands that a text has to be understood from its own context and not from that of the interpreter, is not even mentioned as a basic canon, although various formulations of methodical viewpoints which have been derived from this canon are the target of criticism.[3] The order is exactly the reverse in the philological approach, where it is the first canon which provides the methodical and critical restrictions for projections about signification which develop following the second canon and where it is the first canon which connects hermeneutics with critique.

3. There is a tendency to treat various other forms of methodical and premethodical understanding, such as psychoanalysis, ideology critique, and even **phronesis** under the heading "hermeneutics." Seen from the viewpoint of the philological-historical method, such extensions are either dubious or useless metaphors.

For philology and history as a research activity, philosophical hermeneutics is an exuberance without real practical value, and sometimes it is even dangerous. Both disciplines are, however, not able to provide arguments in their defense. Philosophical hermeneutics has thematized a level in the problem of understanding which is, according to conscious methodologists, presupposed by the method.[4]

---

1. The reader who is interested in bibliographical material can check T.M. Seebohm, "The Problem of Hermeneutics in Recent Anglo-American Literature," Parts I and II, PHILOSOPHY AND RHETORIC, Vol. 10, pp. 180-197, 263-275.

2. The most extensive bibliography and collection of historical material about the two canons are given by E. Betti, ALLGEMEINE AUSLEGUNGSLEHRE ALS METHODIK DER GEISTESWISSENSCHAFTEN, (Tuebingen, 1967), p. 216 ff. Betti, following Schleiermacher, lists the critical canon as the first canon and the canon of the whole and the parts as second canon. In the survey mentioned in note 1, I listed the canon of the whole and the parts as the first, because this canon is the only one mentioned in the recent literature in English.

3. H.G. Gadamer, TRUTH AND METHOD, (New York: 1975), p. 356; P. Ricoeur, INTERPRETATION THEORY, (Fort Worth, Texas), 1976, pp. 92-93.

4. A. Boeckh, ON INTERPRETATION AND CRITICISM, (Norman: 1968), pp. 46, 49.

The immediate subject matters of the method are documents and traces. The task is to develop an objective and correct understanding of these objects, i.e. to remove misunderstanding and not-understanding. The method presupposes that languages are known and can be learned in the fourfold aspects of speaking, listening, reading, and writing, independently from the method. The method presupposes, furthermore, that documents and traces (although not necessarily the ones which need extensive investigations) are already understood in the premethodical realm of the **living tradition,** i.e. that it is known what it means to understand documents, and that some documents are understood. The methodical approach presupposes the living tradition because it is the realm in which unmethodical understanding produces a steadily growing realm of misunderstood documents and documents which are no longer understood at all. It is in the process of unmethodical understanding that the possible tasks for the methodical understanding are produced.

Methodologists of the nineteenth century were well aware of this situation. In their terminology it holds first that the general realm which has to be presupposed is the realm of all elocutions, i.e. interpretations in the sense of Aristotle's **"De Interpretatione."** Regarding the process of understanding, in general, regardless whether methodical or not, one has to distinguish between the **elocutio** or **interpretatio** of the text about a certain subject matter and the **elocutio** or **interpretatio** given by some interpreter about the text and what the text wants to say. The latter is called **explicatio,** its most simple form would be a commentary on the text. The mediating factor between **interpretatio** (1) and **interpretatio** (3) is interpretatio (2), which is **translatio** in the broadest sense, i.e. including the translation from one language into the other as a special case as well as the **translatio** as the mediating activity which keeps a tradition alive. The whole structure,

interpretatio (1)	interpretatio (2)	interpretatio (3)
elocutio (1)	translatio	elocutio qua explicatio,

is a specific structure of communication through language which occurs if there is written speech. Written speeches as texts belong to the realm of **elocutio (1).** Speeches, referring to texts, be they written or oral, belong to the realm of **elocutio (2).** The method refers to the mediating process of **interpretatio (2)** alone, i.e. to **translatio.** Hence it presupposes the general structures of communication in written speech, which is, in turn, embedded in the general structure of language as a means of communication.[5]

The new philosophical literature about hermeneutics develops its conceptions of hermeneutics as an analysis of living literal tradition in general, i.e. includes the aspects in the threefold appearance of **interpretatio,** which are not considered by the methodologists, and conflates, in the last instance, the general theory of understanding and hermeneutics with a general theory of language. Regarding methods and methodology the following positions over and against the traditional hermeneutics can be developed:

A. The main focus is the relation between the premethodical realm of a living tradition and the method. The two possible positions are:

    1. The method is considered to be an achievement. The task is to provide a critical justification of its validity. This will be the position of this essay.

    2. The method is considered to be a degenerated form of understanding. Understanding in a living tradition is the authentic form of understanding. The claim for validity and validating procedures maintained by the method has to be rejected.

B. Since the living tradition belongs to the lifeworld and a manifold of methods can be developed here, the philological method is not the only method of understanding. A general hermeneutics has to consider them all. Two alternatives under this viewpoint are:

    1. The development of a general hermeneutics which includes all dimensions of methodical understanding in one system. The philological method has a legitimate place in this system and is methodologically prior to all others.

    2. The claim is that other methods lead far beyond the philological-historical method and offer a more scientific and deeper understanding. The philological approach has to be criticized for its methodological inconsistencies.

The Need for a Phenomenology of Communication

The following approach to the type of communication which takes place in philological-historical interpretations and its presuppositions will be phenomenological in the Husserlian sense. It can be admitted that the approach of positive

5. Boeckh, l.c. pp. 47-48.

phenomenology has been criticized by modern philosophical hermeneutics. This critique and its possible refutation is not the concern of this paper. What has been said about hermeneutics by authors who are more or less representative of philosophical hermeneutics can be understood, at least in part, as positive phenomenological analysis and can be criticized as such. It is necessary for present purposes, to bracket the deeper concern of philosophical hermeneutics about "being," "truth," and "authenticity." What is left can be used either as an element of positive phenomenological analysis or as descriptions which have to be corrected or completed by such an analysis.

Phenomenological investigations about methods in general thematize three constitutive aspects. (1) Every methodical approach is onesidedly founded in a specific premethodical realm which already has its own procedures for making something evident. The structure of these procedures determine the possibilities of the method. (2) Every method implies one or more idealizations. To characterize a method means first of all to determine the idealizations it implies. (3) Every method leads to some abstractive reduction. Geometry can serve as an example: (a) The premethodical realm is the realm of visible objects. It is possible to distinguish in this realm different shapes of objects and to classify them as curved, straight, having angles or not. (b) We have a method at the very moment in which some of these objects are defined in terms of idealizations, e.g. "a straight line is the **shortest** connection between two points." Such idealizations cannot be represented in the premethodical realm in a perfect fashion. (c) Given these idealizations the discipline is constituted as the discipline of a realm which is the result of abstracting from all properties of corresponding objects, given in the premethodical realm, which cannot be explicated in terms of the idealization.

Note that (2) and (3) imply each other. Note furthermore that it is not necessary for a method that all of its objects can be constructed with the aid of the basic idealizations. In this case one has a discipline which can be axiomatized and formalized. It is sufficient for a discipline to be able to subsume the subject matters of the premethodical realm in some way. Thus, in the general concept of experimentation, we have the probably never fulfilled idealization of the determination of all preconditions. A variety of materials can be subsumed under this ideal. The methodical idealizations of the philological-historical method are of this type, though they have nothing in common with experimentation. The methods of the natural sciences and the human sciences are different, first of all because the premethodical realm they refer to is different.

The remarks in section 1 have determined the premethodical realm of hermeneutics as a method in a vague manner. It is the living tradition. It can be expected, furthermore, that the methodical idealization will be embedded in the two basic methodological canons. The second canon, however, taken alone, is not a promising candidate. Two reasons can be given for this assumption. (1) The second canon was recognized as a principle of interpretation before the philological-historical method was developed. (2) The second canon is accepted as the principle of authentic understanding by those who have doubts in the very possibility of objective and methodical validation of interpretations.

Following the vague guidelines given by the traditional formulations of the first canon, it can be said that they all aim at the possibility of separating the context of a text from the context of the interpreter, an entity which has its own identity. This identity, in the degrees in which it can be fixed, is the same for all possible interpreters of the text. The canon here can be called the critical canon, because any projection about the signification of a text or a part of it can be critically checked and refuted if it is inconsistent with the context of the text, if it is, in the broadest sense, anachronistic. Thus the philologist can point out, e.g., that it is false to assume that a writer of the Attic period refers with "idiot" to a stupid man, because in his context "idiot" refers to a man who does not participate in the political life. Furthermore, philological critique, the counterpart of philological hermeneutics, is based on the first canon, i.e. that the context of the text is an entity which has an identity of its own. According to the classical formulation of Boeckh, the critical question in general, i.e. on all levels of hermeneutics, is about a relation which something has to something else in **its context**, not in the context of the interpreter.[6]

The weakness of traditional hermeneutics lies in its formulations of the first canon. They are vague and misleading. The canon will be an easy prey for its critics if the context of a text is thought to be determined by "the contemporary addressees of the text" or "the original intention of the author." I disregard the different criticisms of these formulations which have been offered by Gadamer and Ricoeur, among others. I offer another, strictly methodological criticism. Such formulations presuppose (a) a knowledge about contemporary addressees and (b) a knowledge about the author's intention.

6. Cf. Boeckh, l.c. pp. 121 ff.

How can such a knowledge be given? Obviously only by texts and traces which in turn need interpretation. The formulations beg the question. They refer to knowledge which can be pre-supposed only if the canon can lead us to alien contexts as identifiable entities, separated from our context. What is necessary is a phenomenological analysis of the premethodical realm of living tradition where the idealization, implied in the canon, is performed. Characteristic for living tradition is that it implies written discourse. **It is hence the analysis of the specific structure of communication in written discourse which has to reveal the possibility of the idealization of the method.** It is the thesis of this paper that modern hermeneutics has either glossed over the differences between oral and written discourse or delivered an analysis of both which is incomplete, not sufficient to justify the idealization implied in the method. What is essential are the **different** possibilities to achieve understanding and work away misunderstanding and not-understanding in oral and written discourse. They are grounded, in the last instance, in something as trivial as the descriptive difference of the sign matter.

Understanding, Misunderstanding, Nonunderstanding in Oral and Written Discourse

The following characteristics of oral discourse are chosen because they are significant for the difference between oral and written discourse. The descriptions are of increasing complexity and presuppose each other in the order in which they are presented.

1. Because of its sign matter, oral discourse presupposes a common time-space field of the participants. This holds for visible gestures as well, which may accompany oral discourse or, in the extreme case, substitute for oral discourse.

2. Past discourse in oral communication cannot be given as the same again. Furthermore, there is no possibility to decide with intersubjective evidence whether a repeated past discourse is really a duplicate of that discourse. What has been said in the past is (a) stored in the **subjective** memory of the partners and (b) this memory refers to different aspects of the discourse: One partner remembers what he has said, the other what he has heard.

3. Oral discourse is directed towards future agreement or disagreement. Both have to be understood in the broadest sense. A proposition is uttered waiting for agreement or disagreement in the narrower sense. Agreement in the case of a command is the performance of an action, and, in case of a question, an answer. Disagreement is by no means the

end of communication in oral discourse. Communication stops only if one partner does not respond at all. Since he will be open for further messages (physical attacks to win back his attention and response included) as long as he remains in the common time-space field, he has to leave this field if he wants to stop communication once and for all.

4. The reason for the undecidability of certain expressions reflecting past speech acts is the specific temporality of oral discourse. Thus

"I have not said this at all. What I said was...."

uttered by the proponent, P, must be accepted by the opponent, O, or else the topic of the dialogue will be dropped and the new topic of the discussion will be the undecidable question what P said. If O chooses the latter direction, P can take advantage of the undecidability with the declaration that his subjective memory has failed. Such a declaration has the same effect as the decision of O to accept what P said and to admit the possibility that his memory has failed immediately after the utterance of P. The declaration is of the type:

"If I really said that, then I did not mean it. What I wanted to say was...."

Such an utterance has to be accepted by O if he wants to discuss the subject matter with P at all. If O rejects it, he rejects the credibility of P as a partner in the dialogue and may as well leave the room.

The utterance "I did not mean it this way. What I meant was...." is undecidable in an even higher degree. P remembers what he said and meant, O remembers what he heard and understood. If O does not accept such an utterance, he implies that P lies and wants to distort communication, an assumption which itself distorts communication about the subject matter. Again P or O or both may as well leave the common time-space field.

5. The utterance "I did not mean it this way" of P is the indication of the discovery of misunderstanding. Misunderstanding can only be discovered by P as a misunderstanding of O. On the other hand, nonunderstanding of O can only be discovered by O himself. It is communicated to P by uttering

"What do you mean by...."

The discovery of a misunderstanding by P in O implies, however, that there **was** a nonunderstanding of O, which was not discovered by O. In some past phase of the dialogue, O, determined by his own system of significations, substituted his understanding of a phrase of P for what was meant by P but was not understood by O. Working away misunderstanding means, therefore in the last instance, working away nonunderstanding. This will be always the task of the proponent. The efforts he must make will (1) transcend what he has uttered and (2) seek elements in the signification system of the opponent which can serve as building blocks of an explanation of what he meant.

6. The last resort of working away nonunderstanding for the proponent are the referents of speech in the common time-space field, including the possibility that he can take O with him to show him something or to involve him into an action. Even if one does not share the thesis that there is a realm of a prelinguistic understanding—though I am inclined to accept it—it must be admitted that common nonlinguistic entities are in the common time-space field of partners in an oral communication.

What is said in (3) to (5) can be illustrated by some models.

Model 1

> P: Christianity is superstition.
> O: That is nonsense and I am not going to discuss it, especially because P apparently likes to hurt other person's religious feelings.

This final fragment corresponds to (3). What O claims in general is that P is not a viable interlocutor for the subject matter, a result, which occurs as the final consequence of the dead end phases of model 2, 3 and 4.

Model 2

> P: Christianity is superstition (as understood by O)
> O: That is nonsense.
> P: I have not said it is superstition, I said it is a superstructure.

Dead end phase (1):

> O: You said it, I heard it.
> P: I have not said it.

Dead end phase (2):

> O: You said it, I heard it.
> P: May be, but this was not what I meant. I wanted to say it is a superstructure.
> O: I don't believe you!

Creative continuation:

Agreement/disagreement—O understands, agrees or disagrees. If he offers in his disagreement some positive proposal, the roles of proponent and opponent are exchanged. A second possibility is: O discovers not-understanding.
    O: What is a "superstructure?"
P has now to work away non-understanding until he finds some explanation which does not trigger the reaction "I do not understand" or "What do you mean by...." If this point is reached the agreement/disagreement level is reached.

Model 3

    P: Christianity is superstition.
    O: What do you mean by "superstition?"

Like in one of the possible continutations of model 2, P has to provide explanations until O can agree or disagree.

Model 4

    P: Christianity is superstition.
    O: That is not the case because there are no magical
       practices in Christendom.

P can now discover in the response of O that O has misunderstood him.

    P: By superstition I do not mean magical practices,
       I mean any belief not grounded in scientific
       evidence.

Dead end phase: O considers this explanation as meaningless. He is not willing even to explore, what P might mean.

Creative continuation:

Agreement/disagreement—If O disagrees, he can give some explication of what he means is implied in the proposal of P, e.g.

    O: There is some scientific evidence, because logical
       derivations can be drawn from articles of faith.

The dialogue can shift, in this case, back to the point in which P discovers that O misunderstood him, now regarding "scientific evidence," or it can shift into model 3: O discovers not-understanding and asks:

    O: What is scientific evidence?

The models as well as the remarks (4) to (6) above are one-sided. At every point of a disagreement opponent and proponent can, for the sake of continuing communication, change roles; for instance if the opponent offers some alternative which is of interest for the proponent and the proponent may, because he discovers some not-understanding on his side, try to clarify it in taking the role of the opponent. Furthermore, the role of the opponent in phases of working away not-understanding is by no means passive. He can force, like Socrates, the proponent to develop his signification system, i.e. to find accounts he never thought of before. Since he can get in difficulties and inconsistencies, the opponent might, at such a point, take over the role of the proponent and try to find explanations based on his signification system. In a functioning dialogue, the goal will always be to reach phases of agreement or disagreement. Taking into account that both partners may switch roles in the dialogue several times, and that they develop signification systems creating them, it can be said that in the dialogue they develop a signification system which is supposed to be intersubjective for each phase in which they can ask themselves for agreement and disagreement. In an oral dialogue there really is a fusion of horizons and understanding presupposes such a fusion. It may be added that, in the most rational case, the result can be a scientific terminology.

It is, however, doubtful, whether such a result can be reached with the aid of oral discourse alone. The question is what happens in a community in which written discourse is not available. A rigid abstractive reduction, which is not easily performed, is necessary to answer this question. Since there are no documentations of past speeches and especially those in which somebody utters explanations about what he meant with this and that phrase, they are not identifiable and will be forgotten. From case to case, depending on changing situations, new patterns will be generated out of unidentifiable old ones which serve as debris, as material for bricolage. Neither a signification system of the past nor the signification system of an individual, as different from the systems of others, can be identified in the **savage mind.** Both are of indefinite plasticity and redefinable if necessary in the vital interest of the community. Ethnology provides us with examples.[7]

7. Cf. for instance Napoleon A. Chagnon, Yanomamo, PRIMITIVE WORLDS: People Lost in Time, National Geographic Society, 1973, p. 145. The "extravagant public manipulations of events" necessitated by the wish to make peace mentioned here, or better a new coalition, are surprising only for a member of a culture based on written discourse. Our own politicians would probably be inclined to give reinterpretations of the past as often as they think it to be useful. They are careful about it because there are written documents and, nowadays, even tapes. The free reinterpretation of the past is unlimited and checked by nothing in a culture which knows only oral discourse. Who in a tribe is going to challenge with his subjective memory what has been determined to be the past by two chiefs?

It will turn out that the onesided consideration, in which the proponent and the opponent do not change roles, is completely sufficient for a large part of written communication. Leaving out the question whether the opposition "proponent - opponent" can be applied to them, text and reader or interpreter cannot switch roles. Reading and writing co-represent a structure which is in principle different from the one which is characteristic for oral discourse. This can be shown following the list of characteristics given for oral discourse above point by point.

1. Written discourse, because of its sign matter, does not presuppose a common time-space field if it is used as a channel of communication. On the contrary, it is able to bridge gaps between different time-space fields. This is characteristic for written speech, which uses visual signs, and holds as well for all modern means of communiation which fulfill in addition to (1) what is said in (2).

2. Written discourse can be identified as identically the same, again following the same criteria which allow us to identify visible and tangible things as the same. Though there may be doubts from case to case, whether it is the same document, there are criteria of an intersubjective validation of the identity, not subjective memory only. Since this is the case, a written message can be duplicated and reproduced. Whether and how far the reproduction corresponds to the original can be checked intersubjectively (1) plus (2) yield the possibility that a written message can reach an indefinite number of foreign time-space fields.

3. Written discourse is not directed at the immediate future waiting for response, but towards many future contexts, which are all separated from the context, i.e. time-space field, in which the message is written.

4. What has been written, in distinction to what has been said, can be immediately decided. One needs witnesses in court and their subjective memory to get some evidence of what has been said or promised. The written document is, in the contrary, able to speak for itself.

5. No written message, no text, is able to discover that it was misunderstood and to utter "I did not mean it this way." Every library would be a terribly noisy place if this would be the case. No text, furthermore, is able to continue itself, if a reader utters: I do not understand.

6. Since there is no common time-space field there are no immediate referents for the sender and the receiver of a

written message. Hence this medium is no longer given as a last resort for difficulties in understanding.

The Living Tradition and the First Canon

Since written discourse can replace oral discourse it is natural to consider living tradition as some extended dialogue in which the text functions as a proponent, the reader as an opponent, both struggling for truth. The lists above, however, show that such an attempt is misleading. What a living tradition is should be considered first on the side of the act of writing, i.e. sending a message, and not so much receiving it. What one knows about the intentions accompanying the act of writing is exactly what one knows about the sender of a written message or an author of a text if one has the text and no other information.

A written message is sent to contexts which are not the context of the writer. He knows that the receiver will get the message in some future, disconnected from its own. I.e. it is through writing and then reading that we not only have an environment but a world. If it is a general slogan, that language determines the limits of our world, it should be added that the limits of a language which is only spoken are narrower than the limits of a written language. A message can be directed to a certain person or a group of persons in such a way that the author can expect that they might send him some reply or else come and see him. Though it might be difficult to determine what a contemporary addressee is regarding a text, everybody who writes knows that in general a contemporary addressee is the one who might send him a reply, even if it is not the addressee one had in mind, e.g. the answer of a husband who intercepted a letter from his wife's lover. A message can be directed, however, to a future, which transcends the world of contemporary addressees and every message, written without this intention, can be received in such futures. A lawgiver addresses all persons in the future of his state, a poet all those who love poetry, etc. The author does not and cannot expect any replies from his addressees, nor does he expect that he will be able to answer their questions. What he expects are reactions of receivers in the future directed towards their contemporaries in oral and written discourse, or even in the same way to the open future as the text he produced. The lawgiver expects the judges to judge according to the law, he expects that their decisions in court will be promulgated and he expects that commentaries directed to the application of the law under changing circumstances in the future will be written. A parallel web of expectations can be discovered for every literary genre of a living tradition, poetry, science, philosophy. The process can be iterated. Somebody can produce a text, which is itself a future oriented reaction to a text, which in turn was already a reaction to a text. Since, as every writer in a living tradition knows, this can be done at the same time by a contemporary author, it follows that everybody standing in a living literary tradition knows it as a web of texts referring to each other in a temporal order. There is no hindrance to considering all the texts available in a living tradition at a certain moment, i.e. just now, under this viewpoint, adding only what one knows about oneself as a reader.

The crucial situation to start with is the one of a direct contemporary addressee of some message, a letter. What is known in receiving the letter is that it was written by someone in a past not accessible to me, who is now in a present, which is not accessible to me either, and that my reply will reach him in a future, for which this, my writing, is not an accessible past and which will probably not be accessible for my future. It is left to the reader to work this situation out for the case of a wife receiving a letter from her husband, who is in great danger on an expedition or in a war. The main point is, that every written document represents us a "past in anonymity which is not ours." That holds even from a document we cannot read. We have only to know or assume that it is a text. What has to be added is only that if the text we read refers to another text, then it represents to us the same temporal relationship we have regarding this text as a relation this text has to the text mentioned in it.

The aspect of reading as well as writing reveals the same general structure which texts connect with texts in a living tradition. Reading a text, T1, which is the message of the original sender and then a text, T2, which can count in some sense as a reply to T1, a commentary, a criticism or even a copy of T1, provided it is a manuscript, then the reader can realize that T2 is in the same relation to T1 as he is to T1 and T2. There are further possibilities. A text T3 can be discovered, related in the same way to T2 and T1, but as well a text T4, which might relate to T1, T3, but not to T2, or to T2, however not to T1 and T3. Furthermore a text may be a reply to different texts, themselves not ordered as messages and replies but speaking to a similar subject matter, i.e. there would be a text, Tn, responding to $Tn-1^i$ to $Tn-1^k$. The general theorem, obtainable from this consideration is, that to every text, T, there belongs a possibly empty set of texts ordered in the form of a branching tree or, to use the philological term a **stemma**.

Some authors, representing modern philosophical hermeneutics, have noticed that a text can be read in different contexts by different interpreters and have pointed out that the reason for this property of written messages is the sign matter. Furthermore they indicated that it is this property of written language which constitutes a world for us, a world of communication which reaches from one time-space field into others. The description is, however, incomplete and the conclusions drawn from it regarding the first canon are wrong.[8] Two further properties, which are derivable from the sign matter and the spatio-temporal pattern of communication made possible by it have to be added in order to explain the basis of the methodical idealization of the first canon.

1. A text can be represented in many contexts of different interpreters **and** many texts are available in the context of each interpreter.

2. Regarding these many texts every interpreter can discover that some of these texts refer to some other texts in the same relation in which he stands to them and would refer to them if he would produce a text which has the character of a reply.

That means, however, that one can distinguish for each text a past horizon, represented by texts which are explicitly or implicitly mentioned in the text, and a future horizon, represented by texts which refer to this text. For instance, reading a text of Kant, the **First Critique**, it is possible, without understanding very much, to notice, that he refers to texts written by Hume, Leibniz, Locke, Wolff, Berkeley and Descartes. They all belong to the past horizon, which is structured, because, e.g. Leibniz refers to Locke, but not to Hume, Hume refers to Berkeley and Locke, Locke to Descartes, etc. A complete reconstruction delivers a **stemma**. On the other hand there are texts, like texts from Fichte, Hegel, Natorp and others which refer to the **First Critique.** The basic idealization of the first canon is the sharp distinction between the past and the future horizon of a text and a corresponding definition of "context of the text." The context of a text is the realm of all texts of its past horizon, i.e. all texts the text refers to, explicitly and implicitly. No historical knowledge about the author is necessary nor any psychological assumption. What is presupposed is a knowledge of the spatio-temporal pattern of communication through written discourse, known to the interpreter as somebody who stands himself in this pattern. He associates this structure with every text **a priori** and this is sufficient for

8. Ricoeur, l.c. pp. 28 ff, 34-35. "Thanks to writing, man and only man has a world and not just a situation. . . . It frees reference from the limits of situational reference."

the constitution of the concept "author" and the identification of an author for the purposes of the first canon.

The transference of the spatio-temporal communication pattern of written discourse leads to a second concept of context of a text. These have not been distinguished in traditional hermeneutics. Writing a text I know, regarding the future horizon, that there will be possible replies, either oral in my future time-space field, or written messages out of other time-space fields, which can reach me in some future time-space field. Written discourse waits for answers of this sort. The second idealization of the first canon, which delivers the concept of the contemporary addressee, refers to a certain segment in the future horizon of the text. It is the segment, in which correspondence dialogues are possible. Their basic pattern is a text, T1, a text, T2, referring to T1 and a text, T3, answering T2 and referring to T1 as a text written in the past by the author of T3. This pattern is a pattern known as belonging to the spatio-temporal communication pattern of written discourse. It is as well known there that answers one expects are not given and that answers one does not expect are given. In releasing the message we cannot determine which other time-space fields from which a reply is possible will receive it. It is the transference of this pattern to every text which constitutes the context of an "author" and his "contemporary addressees." Again, no historical knowledge is necessary for the constitution of this idealized frame, which is the frame of a world of contemporaries. Historical knowledge, derived from texts, can be filled in, as well as concept of context qua past horizon of a text can be filled in.

The methodical significance of the idealizations, leading to the concept of context, are based in the corresponding abstractive reduction. The need for a method, based in the reduction, creeps up in the development of the living tradition itself and is based again in the specific pattern of communication of written discourse. Already in a correspondence dialogue one possibility of working away misunderstanding and nonunderstanding is no longer given. It is (6), the reference to objects in a common time-space field of the interlocuters, which is missing. What is gained, however, is the possibility to decide the question of what has been said immediately and intersubjectively. What is written can be given as the same again in different contexts. The situation changes radically if one leaves the world of the context of contemporary addressees, i.e. considers the reactions to texts which can no longer be answered. If one sticks to the model of the dialogue alone, the result will be that the means to work away misunderstanding and nonunderstanding are completely distorted:

1. Proponent and opponent cannot switch roles. The text is the proponent, the reader the opponent.

2. The proponent has neither the possibility to give the signal "misunderstood" nor the possibility of correcting misunderstanding.

3. The signal "not understood" is not received by the proponent and again he will not provide explanations working away not understanding.

4. In the oral dialogue, the opponent is not able to discover himself misunderstanding.

5. In the case of nonunderstanding, he is forced to provide his own explanations, which will be based on his signification system, i.e. he has to do with consciousness what he did without it in an oral dialogue producing misunderstanding in many cases.

Such a process leads, in a living tradition, to accumulation of nonunderstanding. The guess about signification produces misunderstanding and misunderstanding leads to further nonunderstanding and inconsistencies. The hope to reach a phase of agreement or disagreement which both would be instances of the application of the text in the context of the reader without signification is disappointed. The text will be dismissed as not applicable, meaningless. There is a steadily growing realm of texts which drop out. Cultural revolutions, changes in the structure of the language, can accelerate this process. We are not interested in disputes with people who are not able to explicate properly what they mean in a dialogue. We will stop communication with them as useless. Partners in oral communication, however, can always be forced back in communication on vital questions. This holds, to a certain degree, for contemporary addressees. Contemporaries are those who can or could enter a common time-space-field in which written discourse can be replaced by oral discourse. On the other hand it is easy to dismiss a text. No cooperation with it is necessary, because the text of a living tradition which transcends the community of the contemporaries of the present represents a time-space field to which there is no immediate access.

The transition from not-understanding to the dismissal of a text occurs quickly for the careless reader. The careless reader is the one who relates to texts with the same expectations he has towards a partner in an oral dialogue and will, therefore, be soon disappointed. He is careless because he does not realize the possibilities offered by the sign matter of written communication. A text is a message which can be given as the same again. That means, that the reader, who is making a guess in case of a nonunderstanding, checks this guess as a hypothesis with the aid of other parts of the text, which can be given again, for consistency. The whole of the text serves in this sense as a resource which can give us at least in some cases answers concerning our nonunderstanding. The careful reader is willing to abstract in such cases from the explications which are natural for his context of signification but create inconsistencies in the text. The idealizations of the first canon allows us to widen the realm in which hypotheses, filling in gaps of nonunderstanding, can be checked and falsified or validated considerably. Regarding questions of grammar and lexicography, the context will be formed by the texts which are contemporary to the text in the sense of the definition given above. Regarding questions of specific systems of meaning and reference the context is the set of texts which belong to the past horizon of the text. Any interpretation which is either taken from the context of the interpreter or some text outside the context of the text counts (a) as a mere hypothesis, if neither confirming instances nor counterinstances can be found in the context, (b) as falsified if counterinstances can be found in the text and/or context, and (c) is confirmed in the degree in which confirming instances can be found. The study of the context reveals in addition misunderstanding. Misunderstanding is discovered if a hypothesis which does not hit counterinstances in a text or a large part of the text and even seems to be confirmed by some instances is confronted with counterinstances in the broader context. Just as in an oral dialogue, the discovery of misunderstanding indicates that something has not been understood. Since texts can be given as the same again, a search can be started to find out where exactly the misunderstanding and the corresponding not-understanding is located. A new hypothesis can be introduced and checked with the aid of the determined context of the text.

The abstractive reduction is the reduction from all texts and interpretations which do not belong to the context of the text as valid interpretations. This does not imply that they are invalid. They are neither valid nor invalid, they are hypotheses. Further methodological investigations would have to specify the application of the first canon to different layers of interpretation and different fields. They cannot be discussed in this framework. One further remark is, however, necessary. The abstractive reduction has to be applied to every text, i.e. to the texts in the context of a text as well as to those which have the text in their context. In making these transitions, the method constitutes history and historical signification. Developments of signification and interpretation can be identified.

A phenomenological analysis of the spatio-temporal character of the pattern of communication in written discourse which occurs as such in every living tradition can show, first, that criticisms of the first canon based on observations of language in general are in principle misleading, because they disregard the specific abilities of written discourse to cope with problems of misunderstanding and not-understanding and assume without justification that the merging of horizons, which is necessary in the case of an oral discourse, occurs in the same way regarding written discourse. The phenomenological analysis can show, furthermore, that the methodical idealization implied in the first canon can be developed out of the structure of the pattern of communication in a living tradition without making any psychological guesses or presupposing historical knowledge in a circular fashion. All criticisms of the foundations of the philological historical method raised by the new hermeneutics have to be rejected on the basis of the phenomenological analysis given.

Abject Communication

Alphonso Lingis

One can regard communication simply as the circulation of truths (as well, of course, as deceits, imperatives, optatives, fancies, etc.) formulated in the code.

One can also see in communication a process in which truths are veritably constituted. Recent philosophers such as Buber, Levinas and Wittgenstein have tried to show how truth requires a nonrepresentational relation between one speaker and another, and not only a relation between a representational mind and the world.

It is often thought that phenomenological and existential philosophy has brought to the fore a thematics of intersubjectivity and communication. But in reality the most forceful elaborations contributed by these thinkers have exhibited a process of degradation and dissipation of truth in its very communication. Against the themes proper to dialectical philosophy showing certainties formulated in moments of individual insight being fixed and confirmed as truths through communication, promoted to the register of the universal, and against the positivist views of truths formulated in individual insights being progressively accumulated and fitted together with the abiding stock of what had already been received, these thinkers thought they saw insights suffering an emptying out through the process of becoming common. Not only do they suffer a loss of meaning, but they begin to function as falsehoods.

That is why there could be, at a time when scientific civilization is accumulating and assembling its verifications with

INTERPERSONAL COMMUNICATION: Essays in Phenomenology and Hermeneutics, ed., Joseph J. Pilotta, Copyright 1982, The Center for Advanced Research in Phenomenology, Inc. and co-published by arrangement with The University Press of America, Inc.

a purpose and an assurance as never before, a crisis affecting the very foundations of science--and even of mathematical science. Husserl inaugurated phenomenology as the procedures his search for the meaning of arithmetic traced out; at the end of his life his phenomenology was investigating the origin of geometry.

The crisis, as Husserl analyzed it, is both a loss of meaning and a falsification. The mathematical sciences stand as perhaps almost fully elaborated and certainly internally consistent systems, but their referents lie in uncertainty and dispute. What is the region of objects of which these sciences constitute knowledge? Do all these symbols really symbolize realities? But this uncertainty as to significance affects the whole body of the mathematized natural sciences. Disputes between idealists and realists are as far from being settled as ever. "Mathematics and mathematical science, as a garb of ideas," Husserl writes, "or the garb of symbols of the symbolic mathematical theories, encompasses everything which, for scientists and the educated generally, represents the life-world, dresses it up as 'objectively actual and true' nature."[1] This garb of symbols "dresses up" the fragmentary and discontinuous data of natural experience--but when fully worked out, the scientific representation of nature can no longer be said to resemble the spectacle of what natural experience takes to be reality. Its own coherence and consistency contests the reality-claim of that experience. But what can be the validity of positing this very tissue of symbols in reality? In doing so are we not simply making it correspond to a purely noumenal X?

Phenomenology then is inaugurated as a program of recovery of the referents of sciences which have come to subsist as pure systems of symbols. The slogan "Back to the things themselves!" means first a search for the original insights that saw what was first formulated in the mathematical concepts of unity, multiplicity, part and whole, line, plane, volume, etc., that first "gave" these givens, these formal objects, these properties and relations between entities of the form of "objects in general." Every symbol first received meaning in a moment of insight, where there was evidence, visibility, of something given. Symbols can be repeated, and combined, according to formal rules, without these moments of living insight being reactivated. But in this repetition, this purely technical operation with symbols, the insights, and what they give, can be lost. The reinstatement of the referents of the system has to be an individual performance, for every insight

---

1. Edmund Husserl, THE CRISIS OF EUROPEAN SCIENCES AND TRANSCENDENTAL PHILOSOPHY: An Introduction to Phenomenological Philosophy, trans. David Carr (Northwestern University Press, 1970), p. 52.

that gives reality is a mode of consciousness in the first person singular--an "I see..."

The formal objects, objects of the form "object in general," form the region of reality known by mathematical science. The other sciences also delimit regions of reality. The search for those regions, the reactivation of the insights that originally give the givens mathematically symbolized, "dressed up," by physics, chemistry, anatomy, biology, psychology, etc., is what Husserl named the phenomenology of the life-world. The spectacle of the life-world, constituted in natural perception, is not a purely subjective, private or immanent representation, nor is it an obscure and indistinct apparition of reality, whose clear and distinct version is brought into focus in the mathematical "garb of symbols." It is the primary apparition of original reality, which has to be reinstated as the original and ultimate referent of the body of sciences.

The crisis of the sciences in the twentieth century is also the discovery of a falsification. Husserl locates this falsification in the naturalization, the objectification, of the mind. The mind, as the set of intentional operations which give objects, is taken to be a set of objects themselves subject to mathematical calculation, subject to the laws that regulate mundane objects generally. This produces empiricist psychology, whose spurious scienticity is evinced in the dubious character of its measurements and the inauthenticated character of its few laws. In addition every degree of credit conceded to it in fact undermines the whole ediface of objective science of which it aims to be the final part. For in the very measure that it formulates mental operations and performances as objective events regulated by the universal determinisms of mundane reality, it makes unintelligible the mental operations that produce valid representations of reality, and that produce in particular the symbolic systems which the sciences are, making unintelligible the truth-value of every science. Progression in the elaboration of empiricist psychology means foundering ever deeper in the crisis of scientific rationality.

But empiricist psychology, and empiricist treatments of other mental performances such as institutional history, sociology, jurisprudence, etc., which Husserl does not hesitate to label systematic falsification, are not really the locus of the trouble. The problem is more general and more deep. There is a process of emptying out of meaning and of falsification which begins as soon as the communication of the dator intuitions, the insights, always in the first person singular, which give objects, occurs.

Husserl elucidates this by analyzing a mathematical system. At the beginning of a mathematical system there are insights, insight which constitute, which give, mathematical objects, objects in the form of "object in general." This corresponds to the passage from the pregeometrical art of surveying to the constitution, via abstraction and idealization, of ideal objects such as (pure) line, (perfect) circle, (infinite) dimension. It is these objects which are documented by the symbols.

But these symbols which have (intuitable) content have also formal relations. The deductive science of formal geometry is invented when it was discovered that truths concerning the properties of and relationships between objects just taken as "objects in general" can be formulated by studying the purely formal relations between the symbols. A pure calculus on the formulas can deductively produce a formula which will have truth for the mathematical objects if the formulas from which it was deduced had truth. The calculus dispenses with the insights. And because it does, a mathematical discipline can achieve the completeness of a perfect science—containing the totality of all possible truths regarding the properties and relationships of the objects of its region of reality. It does not have to await the impossible accumulation of the insights giving each of those objects, properties and relationships. It can precede piecemeal intuitive knowledge as an a priori and absolute science. One can progress toward more and more complex truths via more and more complicated deductions because once one has "seen" the evidence for one theorem one can subsequently employ it purely calculatively, without reactivating that evidence anew.

There is a necessary detachment from intuition not only during the deduction, but also at the conclusion. At the end of a complex deduction one "sees" that the conclusion is valid, and one proves it by a reversed calculus. But the concluding formula formulates truths regarding the properties or relationships of complex idealized objects for which an adequate intuition is not immediately possible. To see that objective complex one would have to genetically decompose it, returning finally to the elementary insights out of which it was composed.

But such a return to the intuitive bases of the system is nowise required for mathematical work. Practicing mathematicians operate with the system calculatively; they are "technicians" of a sort of "apparatus," a "machine."[2] This

2. Ibid., p. 52.

technical possibility of the symbolism is precisely the secret of its productivity, both of the possibility of working out a priori all the possible theorems legislating an ontological region, and of the possibility of employing the calculations for diverse regions of mundane nature.

It is the fixing of the symbol that makes both a separation from the living insight and utilization of the product of that insight without reactivating it anew possible. When the symbol is reproduced, it, to be sure, reawakens its corresponding significance. But it can do so merely passively. One can remember that one once saw the evidence for the Pythagorean theorem without actually seeing that evidence anew each time one uses that theorem correctly in a deduction.

And it is this kind of passive recall that can be transmitted when one proffers the symbol to another. One can not actually communicate the insight to another; the insight is always a mode of consciousness in the first person singular. All one can do is present the symbol to another, and thus incite in him a recall of having himself seen what the symbol meant, that is, seen what it was it symbolized.

Communication then occurs on the level of the detached symbols, and not on the level of the living insights. It substitutes passive recall for reactivation of insight; it also substitutes credence in the possibility of reactivation for even passive recall—substitutes credence in the possibility of the other reactivating his insight for any insight of one's own. At the limit, a cognitive life that proceeds by communication would be empty of all insight, detached from all immediacy of presence to reality, and finally utterly false, for having lost all sense of reality. This limit is historically produced in the radical scepticism proffered not at the beginning, but at the culminating phase of scientific civilization.

The Heideggerian critique of "talk"—**das Gerede**—diverges from this Husserlian analysis in several ways. **Das Gerede**— acts in the form "It is said that..." The meaning, first articulated in an act, having the form "I say that...," has been reformulated in such a way as to render it common, capable of being communicated, capable of being passed on from one to another without its meaning being affected.

The "talk" does not consist simply of formulas, symbols; it contains an understanding and an interpretation of the world. It articulates the general format of things and the outlines of recurrent situations. It also determines the ways in which one lets the world concern one—one's moods. But Heidegger emphasizes vehemently the function of this very articulation to cover over reality—the each time singular reality, the particular layout of concerns of one's once-only **situation.** Yet does not everything one says have to get formulated in the generalities of language? And do not the generalities of language intersect to articulate where one's own situation lies? This ambiguity is characteristic of talk; all talk equivocates, setting forth one's own situation as equivalent to that of anyone.

Whereas Husserl had seated this extinguishing of the light of personal insight from symbols in their power to awaken a merely passive recall of having had an insight into what they mean, Heidegger seats it in an active existential structure. "The talk" is not a multiplicity of formulas that circulate of themselves; it is a set of recurrent speech acts proffered by speakers who make themselves equivalent to and interchangeable with one another. Inauthenticity— anonymity—is existing as "one," "another one," "anyone"; it is dealing with a circle of concerns equivalent to and inter- changeable with those of anyone else, it is "doing what there is to be done," and saying in one's turn "what one says." And this anonymity is primary: one is "a man" before one sets out to become "oneself." One takes up the talk before one speaks in one's own name.

And this is due neither to myopia nor weakness of will or of ego; it is due to fear of the sense of mortality. If one does not confront the sigularity of one's own real situation and the singular configuration of implements and pitfalls in which one's own death is lurking, and seeks rather to drift over the world, if one does not speak to articulate the singular predicament that sustains and threatens one's own unprecedented destiny, but speaks to communicate with the general lines of things and the recurrent patterns of events, this uprootedness is anxiety; one is speaking in order to not let one's voice and one's concerns die away, one is speaking out of fear of anxiety. One can find and one seeks not certainty, but assurance in the formulas, in the talk that gets passed on.

To find the word that can be true, the speech act that re- veals, it is necessary to withdraw from the talk into reti- cence, into silence. Into the silence that answers not to another, always there, but to the silence of death, even now imminent. Out of this silence can begin a speech that begins to articulate the world for oneself, to articulate one's own singular situation, for oneself. This speech articulating the singular situation, and not the common talk articulating the general lines of the world, can be true—for reality exists in the singular.

For Heidegger the truth-value of a proposition, its revealing function, does not consist in an act of personal intuition, conceived as an immediate grasp of the "thing itself." The uncovering work of an act is itself a temporal process, enlisting various devices and manipulations, including the guidelines of propositions already fixed in the common language. What is essential is that an agency be set up that commits itself to this process—a responsibility. The "I" is this agency, this responsibility. Statements in the first person singular, in the form "I affirm that..," are statements in which an I puts himself forth to answer for what is put forth. Taking what is said and passed about as subject to contestation, he takes the situation his speech articulates as contrasted with that of every other. It is the commitment of himself to answer for the truth-value of his assertion that brings the speaker back to the situation his words sought to formulate. Such is "authentic (**eigentlich**) speech," speech acts that are "my own" (**eigen**), speech acts in which a sphere of ownness, an **Eigentlichkeit**, constitutes itself.

Thus the common speech, the speech become commonplace, become anonymous, speech acts in which the speaker sets himself forth as anonymous, as one—anyone, another one— that says "what one says," has to be reduced to speech acts that are essentially singular and singularizing. Communication is not the norm of authentic speech; Heidegger rather always analyzes what is at stake in authentic speech with the two themes of speech as world-articulating and speech as constitutive of oneself as a singularity. As soon as speech acts get "passed on," get constituted in a form such that they can be passed on, as soon as speech acts are translated from acts in the form "I say that..." into the form "It is said that...," they undergo a degradation. They empty their meaning, they seem now to articulate the general form of the world and no longer only the singular situation of the speaker, but in reality they function now to cover over and conceal the singular lines of reality. And in them the speaker is constituted as a seat of irresponsibility, as a pure material in which anonymous forms of action and of articulation circulate.

In Nietzsche the general forms of thought are bound to general forms of signs—signs essentially structured for communication. And as in Heidegger, the articulation of the world involves a form of articulation of the speaker. Self-consciousness occurs in linguistic signs—in general terms. It is a need. But just what is this need? It is the very articulation of our neediness--our lacks and wants. They are articulated in general terms in order that others may understand them. But from this Nietzsche draws startling conclusions:[3]

1. It is only the "worst and most superficial part of ourselves" that can become conscious. That is, our negativity, ourselves as needs and lacks and wants. And this is the superficial part of ourselves; for life--and this is the very core of Nietzscheanism--is positivity, is force and surplus, an excess of force over and beyond it antecedents, a force that has to discharge itself. Life is not the agitation, the force of need and want in a material mass. Life's own forces are Apollonian and Dionysian, compulsions to dream--to produce visions the world does not give one--and to dance--to move with nonteleological movements. Life is not the agitation, the force of need and want in a material mass. The wants and needs and lacks are surface occurrences; the core of life is plenitude and gratuitous, excess, power.

2. If it is only our needs and wants that get articulated in signs, in herd signals, that is not only because it is only the common form of our impulses that can be understood by the others, but because the others **want** to hear only our needs and lacks. For our needs and lacks are apprehended by the others as appeals to themselves, expressions of dependence on them, declarations of subservience, invitations to subjugation. It is through our needs and lacks that we appeal to the will in the others--the will to power in the others, the will to dominate.

3. It is in articulating ourselves as needs and lacks, in formulating ourselves as negativity, in becoming self-conscious, that we **become** servile. Self-consciousness is a "disease," that is, a becoming-servile, a becoming weak.

These three thinkers have in different ways denounced communication as the determining value of speech. To reinstate the truth-power of speech it is necessary to go back to originating moments in which truth is formulated. For Husserl these are moments of intuitive consciousness in the first person singular--moments in the form "I see..." Husserl does not see any special problem about then formulating what is seen; the symbols in fact were originally given meaning, and thus constituted as symbols, in being assigned to just such intuitive moments. To see the proper, signifying function of a symbol is always in fact to go back to such an intuitive

3. Friedrich Nietzsche, THE GAY SCIENCE, trans. Walter Kaufmann (Vintage Books, 1974), p. 354.

consciousness.

For Heidegger in order to break with the equivocation of the talk, in order to discover what the talk covers over, it is necessary to withdraw into the silence of reticence, to there sense and apprehend the potentialities of the world which the black light of death makes visible, and to articulate these actively, in discursive acts. For this one shall not invent a private code, radically unlike the essentially common terms of the public talk. Rather, one's own singular situation has to be discovered at the intersection of the general lines of the common world, and the speech that articulates and appropriates it elaborated by answering on one's own for whatever is said.

For Nietzsche the best and deepest part of ourselves is the wellspring of utterly positive and utterly singular force that is produced in us and that is felt in the noble and elevating feeling of joy This inner vibrancy Nietzsche opposes to self-consciousness articulated in the terms of the herd code. This self-consecrating feeling speaks to articulate and interpret the world neither in order to shape it for its own predatory needs nor in order to communicate it to others, but in order to give to it the form issuing out of its own force--gratuitously, gift of life to life. That the terms of speech be able to do that presupposes, as Nietzsche indeed presupposes, that the language of herd signals is not original, that the original language, devolving in life out of the music of insects and birds, consisted in judgments of estimation, functioning to consecrate and enhance rather than to communicate cognitive predicates. All the noble words of language first received their meaning in the joyous exclamations "How happy we are! how noble we are! how beautiful we are! how strong we are!" with which the sovereign ones consecrated and enhanced their own compulsions of power. It was these consecrations that they then gave also to things, out of the superabundance of their own vocative power.

The authentic speech can then also communicate itself; but when a communicative intention and function forms speech, the speech degrades and its meaning dissipates. This degradation is not accidental, but essential to the communicative function itself. Husserl has shown that the employment of symbols not only makes possible the eclipse of the living grasp of their meaning, but is itself useful and productive in the measure that the reactivation of the dator intuitions need not occur. And this is not only true for geometrical activity; it is already true in ordinary language.

> It is easy to see that even in [ordinary] human life, and
> first of all in every individual life from childhood up to
> maturity, the originally intuitive life of sense–experience
> very quickly and in increasing measure falls victim to the
> **seduction of language.** Greater and greater segments of this
> life lapse into a kind of talking and reading that is domi-
> nated purely by association; and often enough, in respect
> to the validities arrived at in this way, it is disappointed
> by subsequent experience.[4]

In Heidegger's terms, the terms of speech acts are from the
first constituted communicatively, as commonplaces, in an
original "falling" which is being–with–others. From the first
each agent, each speaker, constitutes himself as equivalent
to and interchangeable with others, and shapes his expressive
gestures in this equivocation. This kind of constituting oneself
first as "a man," "another man," another instance of
unendingly recurring life, has the dramatic existential intent
of evasiveness in the face of death. It is the everyday
affective way to participate in the eternity of life. This mortal
anxiety is the unavowed force which motivates one to frame
all one's utterances as the "common sense," timeless verities,
irrecusable commonplaces.

Heidegger thus shows how there is an ontological pusillanimity
that drives one into commonplace speech; Nietzsche shows how
expressing oneself in the (common) signs of language is itself
what is debilitating and capitulating; each of these utterances
is in fact a call to a subjugating force. For all the instincts
of the servile are to make themselves weak; in all their talk
they ask to be mastered.

4. Edmund Husserl, CRISIS, p. 362.

Index of Names

Apel, Karl–Otto: 1, 17, 32–33, 44.

Aranguren, José Luis: 120.

Aristotle: 137, 143.

Barthes, Roland: 123.

Bateson, Gregory: 12, 13.

Behnke, Elizabeth A.: vii, 91–107.

Berger, Peter: 2.

Berlo, David: 6.

Betti, E.: 142.

Blumer, Herbert: 85.

Boeckh, A.: 142, 144, 146.

Bowers, J. W.: 50.

Brandt, D.R.: 37.

Brummett, Barry: 6.

Buber, Martin: 161.

Bubner, Rüdiger: 25, 30.

Cairns, Dorion: 93.

Cappella, J.N.: 44.

Casey, Edward S.: 78.

Cassirer, Ernst: 114.

Cegala, Donald J. Cegala: vii, 37, 41, 81–89.

Chagnon, Napoleon A.: 151.

Collingwood, R.G.: 134.

Condon, W.S.: 103–104.

Cooley, Charles H.: 117–118, 119.

Crumbin, Nancy Jay: 103.

Dauenhauer, Bernard P.: 103.

Deetz, Stanley: vii, 1–14, 17.

DeFleur, Melvin: 115, 117.

Delia, Jesse: 12, 49.

Descartes, René: 21, 82–83.

Dilthey, Wilhelm: 95, 130.

Doyle, Arthur Conan: 25.

Dreyfus, Herbert: 78.

Ehninger, Douglas: 45.

Eysenck, Hans J.: 88.

Fast, J.: 121.

Findlay, J.N.: 19.

Fink, Eugen: 98.

171

Index of Topics

Contributors

Elizabeth A. Behnke (Ph.D., Ohio University, 1978) is a visiting professor at the California Institute of Integral Studies in San Francisco, has published in the areas of comparative arts and the phenomenology of music, and is currently working on a book entitled, FOR A PHENOMENOLOGY OF INTEGRAL CORPOREALITY.

Donald J. Cegala (Ph.D., Florida State University, 1972), teaches at Ohio State University, has done extensive work in communication instruction, and has authored several journal articles and two books. His research interest is in interpersonal communication competence, and he is currently working on a book entitled PERSUASIVE COMMUNICATION: INFLUENCE IN MASS AUDIENCE AND INTERPERSONAL CONTEXTS.

Stanley Deetz (Ph.D., Ohio University) teaches at Southern Illinois University, has published in the areas of the philosophy of communication and interpersonal communication. He is best known in the field of communication for his article, "Conceptualizing Human Understanding: Gadamer's Hermeneutics in American Communication Research," COMMUNICATION QUARTERLY, Vol.26 (1978). He is currently working on "Critical Interpretive Research in Organizational Communication."

Michael J. Hyde (Ph.D., Purdue University, 1977) teaches at Northwestern University, has authored several articles in the fields of rhetoric, communication, philosophy, and oral history. He is editor of and contributor to COMMUNICATION, PHILOSOPHY, AND THE TECHNOLOGICAL AGE, University of Alabama Press, 1982.

Don Ihde (Ph.D., Boston University, 1964) teaches at S.U.N.Y. Stony Brook, has published extensively in the areas of phenomenology and the philosophy of technology, and has authored several books. Two major works in the philosophy of technology are TECHNICS AND PRAXIS, Reidel, 1970 and EXISTENTIAL TECHNICS, S.U.N.Y. Press, forthcoming.

Alphonso Lingis (Ph.D., University of Louvain) teaches at the Pennsylvania State University, has authored numerous articles in the areas of phenomenological epistemology and the phenomenology of the body. He is the translator of Maurice Merleau-Ponty's THE VISIBLE AND THE IN- VISIBLE, and is currently working on two books entitled SOVEREIGNTY and SAVAGES.

Algis Mickunas (Ph.D., Emory University, 1970) teaches at Ohio University, has authored over thirty-five articles in the areas of hermeneutics, phenomenology, compara- tive civilizations, and neo-Marxism. He has co-authored EXPLORING PHENOMENOLOGY and is currently co-authoring THE PHENOMENOLOGICAL SCIENCE OF COMMUNICATION.

Joseph J. Pilotta (Ph.D., Ohio University, 1977 and Ph.D. Uni- versity of Toronto, 1981) teaches at Ohio State Univer- sity, has published in the areas of phenomenology, hermeneutics, applied social science, and intercultural and cross-cultural communication. He is currently direct- ting a research project, "Assessing Non-Integrative Law in the Black Community" and is working on two books, THE SENSUOUS UNIVERSAL: A CRITICAL PHENOMENOLOGY and THE PHENOMENOLOGICAL SCIENCE OF COMMUNICATION with Algis Mickunas.

Thomas M. Seebohm (Ph.D., University of Mainz, 1962) teaches at the Pennsylvania State University, has authored numerous works in German on German Idealism, hermen- eutics, and phenomenology. His best known work is ZUR KRITIK DER HERMENEUTISCHEN VERNUNFT, Bonn, Bouvier Verlag, 1972.

Hugh J. Silverman (Ph.D., Stanford University, 1973) teaches at S.U.N.Y. Stony Brook, has published over thirty-five articles in contemporary continental thought, philosophy, literature, and philosophical psychology. He has edited PIAGET, PHILOSOPHY AND THE HUMAN SCIENCES, New York Humanities Press, 1980 and is working on SARTRE AND THE STRUCTURALISTS.

Tim L. Widman is a doctoral candidate in the Department of Communication at Ohio State University. He is working in the areas of public interest communication and the interaction of cultural evolution and international com- munication. He is currently translating a volume on the philosophy of culture by the Swiss scholar, Jean Gebser.

This Book
was
composed on
an Olivetti 221 ET.
The Body, Notes, & Headlines
are in
PS Venezia and PS Italic.
The Titles are in
Letraset Palatino and Italic.